THE
MEDIEVAL
QUEST FOR ARTHUR

ROBERT ROUSE & CORY RUSHTON

TEMPUS

Cover Illustration:

King Arthur, miniature from 'Flores Historarium', by Matthew Paris, *c.*1250-52 (vellum) by English School (thirteenth century) Chetham's Library, Manchester, UK www.bridgeman.co.uk

First published 2005

Tempus Publishing Limited
The Mill, Brimscombe Port,
Stroud, Gloucestershire, GL5 2QG
www.tempus-publishing.com

© Robert Rouse & Cory Rushton, 2005

British Library Cataloguing in Publication Data.
A catalogue record for this book is available from the British Library.

ISBN 0 7524 3343 1
Typesetting and origination by Tempus Publishing Limited
Printed and bound in Great Britain

Contents

Preface

This book has its genesis in a session of the International Medieval Congress at the University of Leeds. The authors had been sharing notes on places and things associated with legendary figures, particularly, but not limited to, King Arthur and his knights. During the session, Dr Rushton spoke on the importance of Arthur and some of the objects or relics associated with him for the medieval English monarchy, which was always obsessed with the unity of the British Isles (under their rule, of course). Dr Rouse shared his research into Winchester, a place associated not only with Arthur but also with the putatively Anglo-Saxon hero Guy of Warwick, and with several historical Anglo-Saxon kings. It became apparent during the questions that these topics reflected in each other, and that no book or article since Ditmas in the sixties had really attempted to study these objects and places. When they were discussed at all, it was simply to either confirm or deny the historicity of Arthur, and the credulity or sophistication of the medieval writers who noticed them. This book attempts to bring all of these objects together comparatively, and to speculate (sometimes, perhaps, a little too wildly) about where they might have come from, where they might have gone to, and what role they might have played in the story of the Middle Ages. We cannot pretend to perfection, but we hope our aspirations to entertain and inform have been at least partially met, and that this book will at least in some small way stimulate further discussion of the medieval tendency to 'make real' the legendary past.

List of illustrations

Touching the past: the medieval vogue for Arthurian relics

In his 1485 edition of Sir Thomas Malory's *Morte Darthur*, William Caxton included a preface explaining his motivations for printing the book. He had been asked to do so by several anonymous nobles, whose belief in Arthur was in opposition to what Caxton felt was a growing scepticism. Challenging this rising disbelief in England's greatest historical legend, one of Caxton's anonymous nobles mentions a litany of 'proofs' that Arthur had lived and ruled sometime in the British past:

Fyrst, ye may see his sepultre in the monasterye of Glastyngburye; and also in Polychronycon, in the fifth book, the syxth chapptyre, and in the seventh book, the twenty-thyrd chapptyre, where his body was buryed, and after founden and translated into the sayd monasterye. Ye shal se also in th'ystorye of Bochas, in his book DE CASU PRINCIPUM, parte of his noble actes, and also of his falle. Also Galfrydus, in his Bruttysshe book, recounteth his lyf. And in dyvers places of Englond many remembraunces ben yet of hym and shall remayne perpetuelly, and also of his knyghtes: fyrst, in the abbey of Westmestre, at Saynt Edwardes shryne, remayneth the prynte of his

seal in reed waxe, closed in beryll, in whych is wryton PATRICIUS
ARTHURUS BRITANNIAE GALLIAE GERMANIE DACIE
IMPERATOR; item, in the castel of Dover ye may see Gauwayns
skulle and Cradoks mantel; at Wynchster, the Rounde Table; in other
places Launcelottes swerde and many other thynges.

Caxton's preface, and the proof of Arthur's existence cited here, has
been described as a kind of medieval sales pitch; however, these items
and others were taken as proof by many writers before and after the
publication of Malory's book. Two things bear noticing: Caxton (or, if
we believe him, his aristocratic informant), quickly turns to books for
much of his proof, but beyond the written word he points to specific
physical objects: a Round Table, a sepulchre, the imprint of a royal seal in
wax, a skull. It is these last items, and others not mentioned by Caxton,
which are the focus of this book. Most of the evidence Caxton cites
is now gone, the obvious exception being the massive Round Table
which still hangs in Winchester. Further, most of this evidence would
no longer convince anyone that Arthur had been real. What happened
to all of these items? Where did they come from in the first place? Why
were people so interested in relics of Arthur, both in the Middle Ages
and in the centuries since?

The medieval belief in the historicity of Arthur was neither total nor
naïve. Arthur's existence and indeed his reputation, was the subject of
debate at least from the moment Geoffrey of Monmouth, a cleric associated with the court of Henry II, wrote his monumental *Historia Regum
Brittaniae* or the *History of the Kings of Britain*. In this most influential of
medieval narratives (this is the 'Bruttyshe book' mentioned by Caxton),
Geoffrey tells the story of the Trojan Prince Brutus and his descendants,
who settle in the island of Britain, slay its many native giants and found
kingdoms. Fully a third of Geoffrey's book is concerned with Brutus's
most famous descendant, Arthur.

Geoffrey's fellow historians were divided about its authenticity and
reliability. Henry of Huntingdon hailed the *History* as a new source for
the history of the British before the coming of the Angles and Saxons,
exactly the kind of source he himself had struggled and failed to find
for years. On the other hand, William of Malmesbury, who was himself
interested in the figure of Arthur, roundly dismissed Geoffrey as a liar.

His attitude towards the nature of Geoffrey's book can be seen in the following story that he relates: a certain man has been possessed by demons and when a copy of the Gospels is laid upon him he recovers; however, when the holy book is removed and replaced by a copy of Geoffrey's *History*, the demons return in even greater numbers.

Key to both Henry's delight and William's scepticism is the nature of Geoffrey's book and especially the vexed question of where he found his information. Modern scholars wonder whether Geoffrey's book is propaganda or parody, or somehow both at the same time. Geoffrey appears to have been from a Breton family, resettled near their long-distanced Welsh brothers in the Marches and he may well have known Arthurian stories in an oral form: he tells us that the deeds of the British kings 'were handed joyfully down in oral tradition, just as if they had been committed to writing, by many peoples who had only their memory to rely on.' At the same time, his close association with the *literati* of the court of Henry II was a source of both reward (he was made Bishop of St Asaph's in north Wales) and disdain (there is evidence that the Welsh never allowed him to take possession of his see).

If Geoffrey was trying to find a means of reconciling the Welsh with the aggressive Anglo-Norman rulers of England through praise of Arthur, the forebear of the Welsh kings and the political antecessor of the current regime, he failed spectacularly. His book became the focus of intense debates during the Middle Ages, as the various competing powers of the medieval British Isles sought to claim the legends as their own. The English, the French, the Anglo-Normans, the Welsh and the Scottish all produce varying translations and responses to Geoffrey's work.

As mentioned, Geoffrey may have known of oral Arthurian stories, which seem likely to have circulated in all of the Celtic areas which surrounded the English kingdom: Wales, Brittany and Cornwall. Geoffrey himself, however, claims to have had an ancient British book, unknown to his fellow historians but given to him by Walter Map, a fellow cleric and courtier at Henry II's court. Telling the reader that he had failed to find any information about the pre-English kings of Britain, Geoffrey is delighted to receive the mysterious book:

At a time when I was giving a good deal of attention to such matters, Walter, Archdeacon of Oxford, a man skilled in the art of public speaking and well-informed about the history of foreign countries, presented me with a certain very ancient book written in the British language. This book, attractively composed to form a consecutive and orderly narrative, set out all the deeds of these men, from Brutus, the first King of the Britons, down to Cadwallader, the son of Cadwallo. At Walter's request I have taken the trouble to translate the book into Latin ....

This book has never been discovered and its identity is unknown: some scholars argue that Geoffrey used a combination of oral tradition, a book detailing Arthur's twelve battles against the Saxons by the mysterious Nennius and liberal helpings of what might kindly be described as creative invention. Very few believe that there was any specific, single 'attractively composed' book, and certainly Henry of Huntingdon had experienced little luck looking for exactly this kind of source. Arthurian history in the Middle Ages, at least for the world outside of the Celtic areas in which oral legends were remembered and retold, thus begins with a lost object. Many readers will recall that Arthurian storytellers become obsessed with another lost and mysterious object, the Holy Grail, which continues to fascinate and mystify to this day. Arthur's world is always one of loss and hope for recovery.

The English kings accepted the challenge of Geoffrey's book and the literary tradition that it begat and increasingly saw themselves as Arthur's political and even blood heirs. Edward I, the king who did the most to extend England's power within the British Isles through aggressive invasions of both the Welsh and Scottish kingdoms, once wrote to the Pope claiming power over Scotland on the basis of Arthur's conquest of the Scottish, a conquest of which Geoffrey had written. Edward IV and Henry VII both claimed descent from Arthur and much of the Tudor claim to the throne came not from their tenuous relationship with the last Plantagenets but rather from their Welsh descent. It is no coincidence that a number of English monarchs have named their firstborn sons Arthur, and it is only to be expected that the failure of any of these Arthurs to come to the English throne and fulfil the ancient prophecy of King Arthur's return has lent further impetus to the myth itself. A prophecy so obviously delayed by murder and misfortune remains a prophecy waiting to come true.

It soon became clear that books and the stories that they contained were not enough: Geoffrey's useful *History* could not only be ignored, worse still it could be rewritten in a culture with little concept of intellectual copyright or narrative stability. The Welsh, in particular, borrowed from Geoffrey in retelling their own earlier native stories, borrowing names and events to flesh out their own versions; for example, the name of Arthur's mother, Ygerna, makes its first appearance in Geoffrey and only later does it occur in Welsh versions of the story. Scottish historians interpreted Geoffrey in a manner completely foreign to his intentions when they claimed that Arthur had been illegitimate and that his nephews Gawain and Mordred had better claims to the British throne. Very few denied Arthur's existence, but one or two brushstrokes in a newly copied manuscript could change the timing of Arthur's birth and the wedding days of his parents Uther Pendragon and the Cornish duchess Ygerna. The typical practice of medieval chroniclers, when they wished to disagree with an older text, was not to deny the previous claims outright, but rather to undermine or subtly change the details to support their own versions of the past. In the attempt to produce a stable version of the past, it therefore became important to seek and to find, and if necessary to create, physical artefacts of Arthur's life and times: in other words, people searched for Arthurian relics.

The cult of relics in the Middle Ages is well understood. Simply put, the medieval church encouraged the belief in physical manifestations of spirituality. Objects which had been associated with the early martyrs, especially bones, had once been venerated as symbols of spiritual resistance to persecution by the Roman authorities; gradually, they became the focus of ritual designed to bridge the gap between God and man. The saints were intercessors, spiritual ambassadors for humanity, ready to put in a good word for their believers and followers on Earth.

Increasingly, veneration of the physical remains was seen to assist Christian devotion: it became a tenet that the contemplation of the ineffable and unseeable divine could be assisted by solid physical objects. Relics, sacred or secular, are portable *lieux de memoire* (places of memory); they help a pre-literate population to remember the stories and characters found in sacred texts. The portraits of kings and presidents found on a nation's money fulfil a similar, although highly political, function. The earliest medieval relics were relics of the body:

the bones of Christians both known and anonymous were collected and venerated as testimony to the power of faith even in the face of persecution and martyrdom. Soon, the bones of the martyrs would be joined by other objects: clothing, instruments of torture and death, even milk provided by the Virgin Mary which somehow went unconsumed by the infant Christ. Constantine, the emperor who converted the Roman Empire to Christianity, had become interested in the faith because his mother Helena was a Christian. During his reign, it was believed, Helena had found the ultimate relic, the True Cross itself, and splinters from the Cross became a staple in the relic-seller's repertoire. The Holy Grail remained an elusive relic and its location has strangely been 'discovered' more often since the Middle Ages than during them. This was, perhaps, because it was an ambiguous relic: the earliest Grail story, Chrétien de Troyes's twelfth-century *Conte du Graal* or *Perceval*, is unfinished and the Grail not clearly defined as the cup from Christ's Last Supper. Although Chrétien's poem was an influential text, within decades the German poet Wolfram von Eschenbach had decided that the Grail was a mysterious stone and not a cup at all. Perhaps the Grail was more trouble than it was worth, at least until the end of the Middle Ages when stories of its location begin circulating again.

Once a shrine or abbey acquired a relic, it could expect numerous spiritual and financial benefits. A patron saint could protect a church from disease, fire or invasion, as long as he or she was kept happy. Saints were reputed to have never been above punishing the sceptical observer, or any member of the ecclesiastical community who might bring dishonour on the saint's good name: medieval saints' lives were full of such stories, encouraging the belief that the saints took a particular interest in the institutions that held their relics. For the individual, a relic conferred numerous benefits. The first was mnemonic: the relic helped the believer to remember the saint and his or her story and further assisted in the act of prayer. Thinking about the saint was a good way to begin seeking the saint's assistance, a kind of meditation that might lead to help with an illness, a battle, even an unrequited romance.

The cult of relics was also famously open to abuse. Chaucer's corrupt Pardoner tells his fellow pilgrims everything they need to know about the relics he sells:

Thane shewe I forth my longe cristal stones,
Ycrammed ful of cloutes and of bones –
Relikes been they, as wenen they echoon.
Thanne have I in latoun [a brass-like alloy] a sholder-boon
Which that was of an hooly Jewes sheep.

The ridiculous claims the Pardoner makes for this 'holy relic' are reminiscent of a snake-oil salesman: dunked in water, the liquid can then be given to livestock to cure their illnesses or jealous husbands to make them tolerant. That the Pardoner also sells ecclesiastical pardons, documents meant to alleviate the guilt of living sinners but increasingly believed to rescue condemned souls from Purgatory or even Hell itself, reminds us that the abuse of both pardons and relics helped to prompt the Reformation.

Even when the relics were genuine, the extreme interest in them could lead to strange practices: from at least the ninth century, merchants dealing in relics (particularly in the bones of saints) were operating in Italy. One of the most famous, the Roman deacon Deusdona (whose name means the Gift of God) had unhindered access to the catacombs under the city where the earliest Christians had been buried. He regularly raided them for suitable sales items; after all, even an unnamed martyr was likely to have God's ear in Heaven and in any event the anonymous could become a named, known and respected saint by the time the bones crossed the Alps into France. On one occasion, Deusdona even agreed to steal the relics of St Peter and St Marcellinus on behalf of Einhard, Charlemagne's royal biographer. The stories told about relic thefts reflect this trade: if a saint's body was successfully stolen from one shrine and 'translated' to another, it seemed apparent that the saint must have approved the process. In many cases, the saint's new home would produce evidence of the saint's complicity. A dream in which the saint of a shrine communicated his or her desire for relocation to a visiting monk normally did the trick. Perhaps the greatest relic theft in medieval history was the 1204 Frankish conquest of Constantinople, in which hundreds of relics left the Byzantine city only to be relocated to France: Louis, the French king, even managed to get his hands on the Crown of Thorns itself.

If relics associated with saints could be forged, stolen or won through military conquest, we should not be surprised if Arthurian relics could sometimes be discovered in much the same way. From an optimistic viewpoint, a false relic of Arthur or St Peter still pointed towards a kind of truth: even if the Round Table at Winchester or Arthur's Seal at Westminster were not real, they still represented what was an acknowledged truth. Arthur had existed, he had presided over a Round Table and he had used a signet ring to seal documents. Therefore, the item itself still stood as potential proof whether real or not. In an age when the survival rate of documents, furniture and other physical objects could best be described as limited, those objects which did exist stood as guarantors of historical truth. They both were and were not 'the real thing'; and in any event, until the historians and philosophers of the Renaissance began asking uncomfortable questions about historical truth, very few people showed much concern.

It is easy, even tempting, to accuse the people of the Middle Ages of ignorance or deception, or both at the same time. But we must bear in mind that the modern era bears traces of the culture of relics. Angela Jane Weisl has pointed to the similarities between medieval relic hunting and the obsession with sports memorabilia, represented in her work by the baseballs hit by Mark McGwire during his 1998 home run race with Sammy Sosa. Special precautions were taken by Major League Baseball to ensure that various baseballs finding their way onto the memorabilia market were authenticated after a rash of fakes were discovered. Newspaper stories about McGwire began to focus on his generosity, his charity work, the childhood signs of his future greatness, and the extent to which the home run race 'saved' baseball from the lingering effects of a disastrous labour strike in 1994. McGwire was a saviour, which is perhaps not surprising given the close links between American national identity and baseball, which has often been described as religious in nature. Baseball even has pilgrimage sites: the Baseball Hall of Fame in Cooperstown, certainly, but also the field featured in the baseball film *Field of Dreams*, which has no connection with the sport beyond its cinematic one. Its status as a pilgrimage site is every bit as manufactured as Winchester or Glastonbury's status as Arthurian sites.

Close links between heroes and relics, group identity and past icons, did not begin in the Middle Ages. Many societies, perhaps most societies, have believed in some form of ancestor worship that could impart strength from the physical signs of the ancestor-hero's presence. The Greeks reserved a place for hero shrines, places where notable ancestors could be worshipped as a kind of lesser deity, a 'demi-god'. The origin of the Greek cult of heroes is still debated, but it did involve sacrifices and, as with the medieval saint, the Greek hero could help or harm his followers from beyond the grave. The medieval saints cult is, in some sense, a descendant of this type of hero-cult, although the Middle Ages imposed a stricter divide between the holy man (or woman) and the hero. As Maurice Keen writes, churches were sometimes 'the mausolea of chivalry', even for figures far more obscure than Arthur: Sir Alexander Neville's coat of arms, as worn at the battle of Halidon Hill, was kept at Marton Priory in remembrance of him and the stalls of the Knights of the Garter in Edward III's chapel of St George were decorated with their heraldic devices. The link between Christian spirituality and terrestrial valour was only rarely disguised in the Middle Ages and Arthur's grand sepulchre at Glastonbury was not the anomaly it is sometimes thought to be.

Geoffrey of Monmouth's book was considered true because there was no authoritative alternative version and because it seemed to testify to historical reality. It explained things that needed to be explained and because medieval readers realised that there must have been a pre-Anglo-Saxon history, in the light of there being no real alternative, Geoffrey's *History* would do as well as any other and it was a good story to boot. The same rationale applied to the Round Table; one had existed, because tradition and history said so. Therefore, the table at Winchester both was and was not the 'real' table. It was the sign of something true. Geoffrey seems to have used this vague area between truth and tradition to his advantage, and the extent to which his book reflects oral or literary sources containing accurate history, as we understand it, is unknown. Geoffrey tries to explain things: why is Bath called Bath? Because a king named Bladud founded it. Who built Stonehenge, and how? Merlin, through his mysterious arts. This latter story will serve to illustrate the point and furthermore will highlight a historiographical problem in dealing with Arthurian relics.

Geoffrey tells us that Stonehenge was an early example of the British import trade. When Arthur's uncle, Ambrosius Aurelius, is trying to find a suitable monument to commemorate the deaths of 400 British nobles, slain treacherously by the Saxon war leader Hengist at a peace meeting and buried at a monastery near Salisbury, here called Kaercaradduc, he asks Merlin for advice. Merlin suggests bringing the Giants' Dance from Mount Killaraus in Ireland, for no man of their generation could build something like it; if relocated to Salisbury Plain, Merlin tells Ambrosius that it will stand forever. Using a mechanical system that strikes observers as magical, Merlin manages to transport the stones despite their weight and the futile attempt of the local Irish king to stop him. Eventually, Ambrosius and his brother Uther, and Arthur's successor Constantine of Cornwall, are all buried at Stonehenge … perhaps an explanation of the many burial mounds surrounding the stones themselves. Did Geoffrey invent this story, or did he find it told as a legend among the Welsh or the people of Salisbury? Regardless of the story's origins, Geoffrey uses it to explain the origin of a mysterious circle of stones, even if his explanation raises as many questions as it answers.

Despite Geoffrey's Arthurian explanation for Stonehenge, with its overt assertion of British superiority over the Irish and its royal burials, Stonehenge never quite becomes an Arthurian site in the same way that Glastonbury and Winchester do. Perhaps this is the result of Stonehenge's unique position in the English landscape: Stonehenge remained relatively isolated and uninhabited. In contrast, Glastonbury and Winchester were important ecclesiastical and royal sites respectively: there were people there to supplement and advertise any Arthurian connections. Stonehenge remained mysterious; few explanations for its existence seemed to stick to it and its subsequent power over the English imagination resides in that very mystery. Its Arthurian associations were soon forgotten.

Nearby Salisbury, however, did become associated with the legend in some romances: Arthur's last battle with Mordred is said by Malory to have taken place 'uppon a downe besyde Salesbyry', even though Malory will have the wounded Arthur brought somewhat implausibly to a nearby seashore soon after the battle. Further, the adventures of the Round Table knights were said to have been recorded by scribes working in Salisbury and these records were used to write the French *Lancelot* cycle:

When they had dined King Arthur summoned his clerks who were keeping a record of all the adventures undergone by the knights of his household. When Bors had related to them the adventures of the Holy Grail as witnessed by himself, they were written down and the record kept in the library at Salibury, whence Master Walter Map extracted them in order to make his book of the Holy Grail for love of his lord King Henry, who had the story translated from Latin into French.

This Walter Map is the same man who allegedly provided Geoffrey of Monmouth with his 'very ancient book' and who is thus credited with writing the vast French romance. This is, in fact, highly unlikely: Map died in 1209, at least seven years before the earliest accepted date for the *Lancelot* cycle. In any event, such literary trifles were not Map's style; he preferred spiritually instructive anecdotes and his association with both Geoffrey's whimsical *History* and the vast Lancelot romances is, many critics argue, part of a vast joke first perpetrated by the witty and urbane writers present at the court of Henry II.

If Stonehenge/Salisbury fell short of becoming an Arthurian site comparable to Winchester or Glastonbury, it was not alone. Unlike many famous authors, those known as or thought to be Arthurian writers never became the focus of sustained interest or pilgrimage; the kind of devotion shown by visitors to Jane Austen's house in Bath or Beatrix Potter's home in the Lake District was never applied to Thomas Malory or Geoffrey of Monmouth. Monmouth never acquired any Arthurian associations, nor did Arley Kings, where the priest Layamon tells us he resided while writing his English translation of Geoffrey's work. The various Arthur's Seats and Merlin's Caves tell us very little about the medieval Arthurian legend, aside from its popularity, and the Arthurian associations of many of these places in fact turn out to be post-medieval in origin. Only when a site attracted Arthurian relics to itself, and when the location of an Arthurian object attracts the legend to its physical location, does it become of importance to our discussion. The present book does not focus on Arthurian sites, which have been admirably discussed in countless other sources since the time of John Leland and Stuart Glennie, but instead examines the relics of the Arthurian age that were so highly valued by the people of the Middle Ages.

The objects discussed in this book, many of which were mentioned by Caxton, were all used as evidence for Arthur's existence in the Middle Ages and beyond. E.M.R. Ditmas wrote two articles for *Folklore* in the 1970s, in which she discussed many of these Arthurian 'relics', as she called them. Ditmas's work has been instrumental in bringing some of the more obscure examples to the attention of later scholars, but few have pursued the stories of Arthur's crown or Isolde's robe; the objects are usually brought forward by scholars only to prove or disprove medieval belief in Arthur or Arthur's historical existence, rather than from any real interest in the items themselves. But many of these artefacts tell their own fascinating stories. How and why were they made? What happened to them? What parallels can we find between Arthurian relics and other objects in the Middle Ages?

Various historical figures can be found in the pages below: Richard the Lion-heart, Llywelyn ap Gruffydd, Henry V, Piers Gaveston, Thomas Malory. Edward I, in particular, appears directly or indirectly in every chapter; his reputation as an 'Arthurian enthusiast', first noted by R.S. Loomis, has perhaps been overstated in the past, but he clearly was interested in the legends of Arthur and their impact on the historical and political life of England and its neighbours (or subjects, as he himself preferred to call them). None of these Arthurian relics are 'authentic' in our modern sense of the term: none can have any serious role in proving Arthur's existence, but still they are best considered not in academic isolation, but rather as key pieces within the wider scope of British history. Even as we examine the medieval quest for a historical, verifiable Arthur, we will be looking at the people of the Middle Ages themselves, for Arthur is a prominent thread in the vibrant tapestry of medieval culture. Arthur, or at least the shadow of Arthur, is inextricably entwined with politics, faith and society in medieval England.

Winchester, the Round Table and dreams of English Empire

... at Wynchester, the Rounde Table ...

As the most well known of his 'many evydences', Caxton's citing of the Round Table at Winchester is an appeal to the historical authority of what has long been the most recognisable and enduring of Arthurian symbols. Synonymous today with the tales of the Arthurian legends, the table has an equally intriguing story to tell regarding its own origins. Once considered to have been an authentic relic of the Arthurian past, scientific and historical scholarship during the twentieth century has revealed the table to be a medieval fake. Dated most convincingly to the late thirteenth century, within the reign of Edward I, 'Hammer of the Scots', the table is a forgery that seems to have been constructed to take advantage of the popularity of the Arthurian tradition. However, as we have argued in the introduction, the fact that the table is a forgery arguably makes it even more interesting than it would have been had it indeed been a true remnant of some dark age past, for the story of the table is one that is in many ways as fascinating and convoluted as the legends which inspired its creation.

Viewing the table today, hanging on the wall of the Great Hall of Winchester Castle, one is struck by the deeply appropriate positioning

1 Edward's Round Table, hanging on the wall in the Great Hall of
Winchester Castle

of Alfred Gilbert's 1887 statue of Queen Victoria, that great symbol of a later British Empire, below and to the left of the table itself. The origin of the table is connected in many ways with the desire of the medieval English kings to forge their own Empire across all of Britain, making use of Arthur's legacy as a king who ruled across the entire span of these Islands and more besides. We shall see that the table, as a powerfully symbolic icon of the legendary Arthurian Empire, was used by a succession of English kings in order to promote their own imperial aspirations. One can only imagine that Victoria, a monarch so inextricably linked in both the popular and the historical imagination with imperial conquest and rule, would have appreciated the setting: the history of the table itself is one that is linked strongly with imperial desire, pretension and achievement.

In telling the story of the Round Table as a medieval artefact, we must first realise that the table is not simply *one* object. While the form of the table today is well known, it has, over the centuries, taken on a number of guises and appearances, each with its own individual cultural and political meaning. It was first a wooden table, most likely covered with painted leather; it was then hung upon the wall some centuries later; and later still was painted in the decorative scheme in which we recognise it today. Each of these different incarnations of the table has its own tale to tell. The story of the table is one of continuing transformations, in both form and meaning, as the table and the Arthurian legends of which it has always been symbolic of have been appropriated by a succession of medieval rulers for their own ends. The Winchester Table, as an object, has also had a significant impact upon the very legends that created it: it has influenced retellings of the Arthurian legends from at least as early as the fifteenth century, fixing the site of Arthur's court and its central dramas in Winchester.

THE TABLE AT WINCHESTER

The first historical account of what seems to be the Winchester Table is that of the fifteenth-century chronicler John Hardyng. In 1464 Hardyng wrote the revised version of his *Chronicle*, in which he records that: 'The Rounde Table at Wynchestre beganne, and ther it ende and ther it

2 The statue of Queen Victoria in the Great Hall of Winchester Castle, made by Alfred Gilbert in 1887

hangeth yet.' Hardyng provides us with no real description of the table and little detail as to its context other than the fact that it was, by the time he visited it, hanging on the wall. Hardyng's comments on the table provide us not only with the first concrete evidence of its display, but also demonstrate the historical importance that he places upon it. For Hardyng, the table seems to have been viewed as a tangible piece of historical evidence and influenced his understanding of the past in a significant fashion. This is clear from the changes that we can see in the different versions of his *Chronicle* that survive today. In the first of these, the version which he presented to Henry VI in 1457, the final battles of Arthur's reign take place in Cornwall, as found in many other versions of the Arthurian legends. However, in the 1464 recasting of Arthur's final days, Hardyng transfers the action to Winchester. This, we suggest, must have been due to his having become aware of the presence of the Round Table at Winchester, as his comments above denote. The importance of the table as a symbol of the material reality of the Arthurian myths was clearly evident to a medieval historian such as Hardyng and he was prompted to rewrite important details of his historical account due to this new 'evidence' being brought to his attention.

The presence of the Round Table also seems to have made a lasting impression on the sixteenth-century antiquarian and scholar John Leland. During the period from 1539 to 1545 Leland undertook a grand tour of England at the behest of Henry VIII and it was during these travels that he visited numerous sites and objects associated with the tales of Arthur. Leland, it seems, took greatly to heart the historical veracity of the Arthurian past and wrote the *Assertio inclytissimi Arturi Regis Britanniae*, a lengthy and learned Latin tract on the subject. In this text, a vigorous and impassioned defence of the historical authenticity of King Arthur, Leland recalls the presence of the Round Table in the Great Hall in Winchester and cites its existence as proof of Arthur's historicity (as Leland writes the *Assertio* in Latin, it is here figured into English by Richard Robinson, as in his 1582 translation).

At *Venta Symeno* alias *Winchester* in ye castle most famously knowne, standeth fixed ye table at the walle side of ye kinges Hal, which (for ye maiesty of *Arthure*) they cal ye round table. And wherefore? Because neyther the memorie nor felowship of the round Trowpe of Knightes as yet falles out of Noble mens mindes, in the latter age of the world. *Kinge Edward* sirnamed the longe, as fame telleth, made much of that rounde order of Knightes. To those vses was the round table instituted and framed, (if it be worthie of credit) and that it was with three feete made of perfect gold.

To Leland then, as to Hardyng, the table stood as material proof of the Arthurian past.

THE IDEA OF THE ROUND TABLE

Before considering the table as a physical object, we must first ask the question of where does the *idea* of the table comes from? As an idea, the Round Table has become of such integral importance to the Arthurian myths that it seems almost inconceivable to imagine that Arthur could have ever sat at a table of any other shape. However, when we read the first and most influential of the medieval Arthurian narratives, the *Historia Regum Britanniae* of Geoffrey of Monmouth, we find no mention of a table, round or otherwise. Rather we must look to one of Geoffrey's literary descendants, writing in the generations that followed him, for the first appearance of the Round Table. The literary origins of Arthur's Round Table are to be found in the mid-twelfth-century writings of an Anglo-Norman monk known by the name of Wace. A learned and well-travelled mythographer, Wace produced in 1155 a French translation of Geoffrey's *Historia*. This text, the *Brut*, is notable for a number of reasons: it was tremendously popular and influential in shaping the form of the Arthurian legends and, importantly for our purposes, it contains the first recorded mention of the Round Table: 'Arthur made the Round Table, about which the Bretons tell many stories.' Unfortunately, we have no record of what these Breton tales may have been and we are left with only Wace's brief explanation of the origins of Arthur's Table: 'This Round Table was ordained by Arthur so that when his noble fellowship were seated to eat they should all be seated and served alike, and no one before or after his fellow knights. Thus no man could boast that he was honoured above any other, for all were seated alike.' This use of the table, which may seem fittingly egalitarian to a modern reader, is in many ways highly atypical of a medieval story. As we observe from history, art and literature, the medieval world was nothing if not extremely conscious of hierarchy and the proper ordering of things and a royal feast was no exception. There existed intricate and highly regimented orders of precedence in arranging the seating at a feast, with the seating priority being reliant upon the rank and importance of each individual guest. This seating order was part of a visual demonstration of social and aristocratic order, illustrating in a very public fashion the structure of the hierarchy of the ruling elite. Wace's Round Table, then, can be seen as being both innovative and revolutionary in its subversion of the usual modes of hierarchical seating, highlighting that from its very inception the table served to symbolise the equality of the fellowship of Arthur's knights – a theme that has remained central to the legends ever since.

While Wace introduces the concept of the Round Table into the Arthurian tradition, he tells us little, aside from its unusual shape, as to what might have been the table's appearance – this he leaves to later writers. Around the year 1200, an English monk living by the backs of the River Severn, in the 'red stone church' at Arley Kings, translated and expanded Wace's French tale into a lengthy English epic. This monk, Layamon, doubles the length of Wace's story and in the process adds a number of elements to the story of the Round Table. The most important of these is the story that Layamon recounts regarding the table's origin. He tells us that early in Arthur's reign, at a feast held in the presence of both the king and the queen, a fierce brawl erupted over an argument about who should be seated where. This quarrel, which was only halted after the shedding of blood, represented a serious breach of the king's peace. Arthur condemned the instigator of the fight to death, along with all his male kin and ordered their female relatives to have their noses cut off – such was the seriousness of this breach of the peace. In order that these events would never be repeated, a new table was constructed by a Cornish carpenter, light enough to be carried with the court on its travels and round in shape, so that such arguments over seating could never again lead to bloodshed within the court. However, again we find little information as to what the table might have actually looked like, suggesting that in both Wace and Layamon it was the table's egalitarian purpose, rather than what it looked like, that was its most important element.

After this, the literary nature of the table moves into the orbit of the French Arthurian tradition, in the writings of Robert de Boron and the retellings of the Grail narratives. De Boron associated the creation of the Round Table not with Arthur, but with his father Uther and far from being representative of equality, he saw it as symbolising the Trinity and claimed that it was a replica of the table at which Christ and his disciples sat at the Last Supper. Within the French tradition, the most notable characteristic of the table is that it repeatedly changes in shape, size and number of seats from tale to tale and there seems to be no concrete conception of its physical nature or appearance. Rather it is the mystical and symbolic qualities of the table that are emphasised. So, if in the literary sources there seems to be little in the way of a model for what the table may have looked like, then from where does the iconic image of the Round Table arise? While there are numerous – and conflicting – literary descriptions of the size, appearance, number of seats and location of the table in the various Arthurian stories, the image of Arthur's legendary Round Table that has become ingrained in our modern imagination is that of the Winchester Round Table.

THE MAKING OF THE WINCHESTER ROUND TABLE

But why is it in Winchester? We have seen how the *idea* of the Round Table came about and how medieval chroniclers and Tudor antiquarians naturally took its presence to be proof of the reality of Arthur's existence. However, why did it appear in Winchester, as opposed to one of the many other Arthurian sites in Britain, many of which surely had a better claim to being the site of Camelot than Winchester did? The earliest English account of Arthur, found in Geoffrey of Monmouth's *History of the Kings of Britain*, makes no mention of Winchester as the site of Arthur's court and of the Round Table. What then made Winchester seem like a suitable site for the construction and display of the Round Table, and what led to the identification of the city with the site of Camelot?

In the early Arthurian legends, Arthur's court has a largely peripatetic nature. The king and his knights moved from place to place according to Arthur's whims. Many different cities were the site of the various feasts and adventures, without any in particular becoming associated with the mythical Camelot. It is not until the time of Malory, who was no doubt, like Hardyng and Leland, influenced by the presence of the Winchester Table itself, that Winchester becomes identified explicitly as the site of Camelot. Malory himself makes this leap of geographic identification when he writes: 'the cité of Camelot, that ys in English called Wynchester.' Writing in 1470-71, he is the first Arthurian authority to explicitly connect Winchester to Camelot. For Malory, Winchester had become *the* location of Camelot and it appears that the presence of the table was his evidence for this assumption. But what made Winchester an appropriate place to situate the table in the first place? In order to discover why the Winchester seems to have been seen as a suitable place for the table, and hence for Camelot, we need to turn to the history of the table itself and examine the story of how and why it was built and displayed in the city.

EDWARD I AND THE CREATION OF THE TABLE

On 20 April 1290, Edward I held a great tournament at Winchester, which is likely to have been modelled after the fashion of the fabulous tournaments of Arthurian legend. No detailed record of the event survives today, but given the accounts that do survive from other comparable royal medieval Arthurian themed tournaments we can imagine the scene: Edward himself, playing the role of Arthur, presiding over the lists. Eleanor of Castile, his queen, beside him, dressed as Guinivere. Alongside them were various invited dignitaries and guests, including many of the most powerful nobles in the realm. In the lists before them, knights played the parts of various legendary characters competing against each other for the honour of the day: steel and wood clash, lances splinter, heroes are dashed from horses and reputations are forged. The scenario proposed here may sound somewhat romantic to a modern reader and while we have no concrete proof that the tournament was Arthurian in nature, Edward certainly had both the reputation and enthusiasm for such events. In the semi-fictionalised account of Edward's reign produced by the early fourteenth-century Brabançon priest Lodewijk van Veltham, Edward is depicted as holding a number of great Arthurian entertainments, including a tournament and feast in which Edward and his guests played the parts of Arthur and his knights. Although van Veltham's account deliberately sets out to construct Edward as a king in the style of Arthur, it does seem to be recording authentically his engagement with the Arthurian tradition: in the details of the Round Table that van Veltham relates, we can perhaps see reflected the real practices of actual royal entertainments of the period. The pageant of which van Veltham tells is a complex one, in which there are many roles to be played and has what seems to be a structured narrative plot through which the various aspects of the day, from jousts to the feast, are laid out before the participants. This form of entertainment seems far from being a simple occasion and seems likely to have involved the levels of expense and preparation that we find associated with Edward's tournament of 1290.

Edward, as a committed Arthurian enthusiast, seems to have had a great love of Arthurian spectacle and appears to have designed this Arthurian spectacle to celebrate the impending marriages of three of his children: Edward of Caernarfon, the future Edward II, to Margaret of Scotland; his daughter Joan of Acre to Gilbert de Clare, one of Edward's strongest and most loyal earls; and another daughter, Margaret, to John, the heir to the rich Duchy of Brabant. The importance of these marriages to the stability of Edward's kingdom, which was a pressing issue given the fact that he was planning to embark upon a crusade to the Holy Land, combined with his undoubted enthusiasm for the Arthurian legend, seems to have inspired him to hold a grand Arthurian tournament focussed around the idea of the Round Table. According to Professor Martin Biddle and his team, who have over the space of many years carried out extensive study of the artefact, it does seem, in all probability, that the Winchester Round Table was constructed as part of the preparations for Edward's Arthurian tournament. During 1289, the year before Edward's grand tournament, Edward spent the sum of 75 pounds, 8 shillings and 11 pence on refurbishing and repairing the royal apartments in Winchester Castle, a considerable sum for the time. This work included repairing the walls and entrance to the great hall and replacing some of the windows. It seems possible that these improvements were in order to prepare the hall for his visit in 1290 and it may well have included the costs of manufacturing the table itself. There is, unfortunately, no direct mention of the table in the accounts for that year, but given that expenses for a total of 100 man-weeks of carpentry labour was paid, it may be that the cost of constructing the table was subsumed into this total.

So, if we accept the likelihood that the table was made for Edward's 1290 tournament, then what purpose was it made for? And what would it have looked like? An Arthurian tournament, like any royal gathering, would surely have ended with a grand feast, and what better place to hold such a feast than at the Round Table of which Wace, Layamon and the other Arthurian writers spoke so highly? Standing on a central pillar-leg and stabilised by 12 radial legs, the construction of the table demonstrates the sophisticated nature of late thirteenth-century carpentry and engineering, exhibiting similarities in building technique with other large wheel-like structures, such as water-wheels and crane-wheels. Solidly built from English oak, 18ft across and probably weighing nearly three-quarters of a ton when first built, the table would have been an immensely impressive setting for such a grand post-tournament meal and may well have formed the centrepiece of the continuation of the Arthurian themed event. At well over 50ft in circumference, the table would have seated over 20 guests with some ease, allowing for Edward's largess to be shared amongst his most important guests. Small nails discovered around the rim suggest that the table was either covered with some kind of cloth, or perhaps had an attached hanging fringe. Records show that Edward's men purchased four expensive rolls of cloth of gold on the day of the tournament, which may have been used to dress the table in a suitable impressive fashion. All in all, the table would have been a fabulous sight and its Arthurian associations would have been clear due to its highly unusual shape and its novel subversion of the usual hierarchy of seating precedence. We have, however, no evidence that the table was ever claimed to have been *the authentic* Round Table and, given what we know of other Arthurian Round Table events around Europe, it would not have been necessary for Edward to have made any such claims. Rather, it seems that the table's Arthurian symbolism was enough and it was left to writers and chroniclers of later centuries to makes claims for the table's authenticity and its status as a relic of the Arthurian age.

In addition to the preparations that took place in the Great Hall, including the construction of the Round Table, we have further records of the expense to which Edward went to prepare this dramatic re-enactment of the Arthurian legends. As we have seen, the royal apartments in Winchester Castle were repaired and refurbished the previous year, at some large expense, presumably with the king's visit in mind, and in the early weeks of April 1290 we find records that the jousting lists were prepared. In the financial records of Edward's Wardrobe, for that year, we find a record of some 13 shillings and 4 pence being paid to one 'Roberto Dote, magistro fossati iuxta Wynton facti pro torniamento' (master of the earthworks outside Winchester, made for the tournament). The extensive preparations that Edward made for the tournament of 1290 seem to suggest that the construction of an object as large and as expensive as the Round Table was by no means out of the question.

WHY WINCHESTER?

So, we have seen that the table seems likely have been constructed for Edward's 1290 Arthurian themed tournament. But why should Edward have considered the city as an appropriate site for an Arthurian *tournament* in the first place? While Malory sets a number of great tournaments in the fields outside of Camelot/Winchester, prior to his version of the legend Winchester was not considered to have been Camelot: so where might Edward, or his counsellors, have got the idea from? The answer seems to lie in the French Arthurian tales of the thirteenth century, where we find the development of an important literary connection between the city and an Arthurian tournament. The French tales of Arthur were extremely popular amongst the French speaking nobility of England, and Edward seems to have been an enthusiastic patron of such works. While on crusade in the early 1270s, Edward is recorded as giving his copy of *Guiron le Courtois* (a thirteenth-century French Arthurian prose romance) to one Rusticien de Pise (Rusticiano of Pisa), in order that he might combine it with other Arthurian tales to create a huge anthology of the legends. Edward's Queen, Eleanor of Castile, was also a patron of the literary arts, maintaining a *scriptor*, or scribe, in her personal employ to copy and illustrate such texts for her own collection. She also extended her patronage outside of her own household, commissioning the Arthurian verse romance *Escanor* from Gerard d'Amiens. Thus it is perhaps to this body of literature that we should look for an example of such a tournament at Winchester, for if Edward did intend to model the 1290 tournament on the Arthurian legends, he would have wished to have a well-known literary representation of such an event upon which to draw.

In the French narrative *Mort Artu* we find just such a literary precedent. Composed by an unknown French writer sometime between 1230 and 1235, this story begins with Arthur declaring that a great tournament should be held at Winchester for the entertainment of his knights. It is perhaps important to note that in the *Mort Artu* Camelot and Winchester are distinctly different places and it is described as taking two days to ride from one to the other. There is not yet any sense that Winchester *is* Camelot: this association seems to have been produced due to the table's existence, rather than the other way around. In the tale, the tournament acts, as do many in the Arthurian legends, as an opportunity for Sir Lancelot to compete in disguise, a stratagem to which he often resorts, given that his reputation as the greatest knight in the world causes many knights to refuse to enter into combat with him. Arriving at the tournament, having borrowed the arms and shield of a young knight whom he met on the journey, Lancelot sends his squire to ascertain how the battle is proceeding. The squire returns and tells him that there is a general mêlée in progress, in which the bulk of the Round Table knights have joined the stronger side. Lancelot, as is often his wont, joins the weaker side, because there is more honour to be won in doing so. He performs many deeds of knightly prowess, is judged by all as the most impressive knight on display and is acclaimed as the winner of the tournament.

Professor Biddle has pointed out that 'the tournament at Winchester is the great set-piece of the early part of the *Mort Artu*' and suggests that this text, or at least the tradition that it represents, may have provided the underlying rationale for Edward's staging of the 1290 tournament in the fields outside the city. The *Mort Artu* establishes Winchester as an Arthurian site and upon the authority of Arthur himself, who had chosen the city as a site for one of his own tournaments. This literary association between Winchester and Arthur seems to have been seen as enough to suggest the idea that Winchester could be an appropriate city for Edward to host an Arthurian tournament and this is most likely the ultimate cause for the construction of the Round Table in Winchester.

EDWARD I: ARTHURIAN ENTHUSIAST

To the modern reader, the idea of a king of England partaking in such a spectacle may seem just a little ridiculous. Such re-enactments today tend to belong very much the sphere of the mail-clad weekend societies, student role-playing clubs and various other hobbyists and historical re-enactors; the likelihood of witnessing leading members of the royal family donning mail coat and Arthurian-themed tabard seems somewhat slim. But to understand Edward's enthusiasm for such a dramatic performance, we must consider the 1290 Winchester tournament within the wider context and cultural importance of such noble pageants. Arthurian themed entertainments were very much in vogue during the Middle Ages, both in England and on the continent, and royal feasts and tournaments that were modelled on aspects of the legends feature prominently in the accounts of court life. The prevalence of such occasions depended very much upon the ruler who was in power at the time and upon the vagaries of fashion: certain rulers seemed to have been more enthusiastic towards the legends than others and Edward I was one of the most passionate devotees of the Arthurian tales. For Edward, this was no idle entertainment – no self-indulgent manifestation of his own personal fancies. Rather, Edward chose the Arthurian theme for the tournament because he knew what it represented: power, grandeur and, most importantly, imperial ambition. For in Arthur Edward must have seen reflected his own desires: Arthur had been king of the Britons and had conquered and ruled not only England, but also the rest of Britain. Arthur had conquered Edward's old enemies, the Scots, he had overrun the Welsh and had forced the Irish to pay homage. Arthur had conquered and ruled all of Britain and this too was Edward's goal. So by so publicly taking on the role of Arthur at the Winchester tournament, Edward was presenting himself, both to his own lords and to his important foreign guests, as equal to Arthur, as not just a king of England but as *Rex Britanniae*. By appearing at the tournament as the legendary king, Edward was demonstrating to the world that just as Arthur had conquered all the peoples of Britain, so would he.

Leland observes, in his description of the table, that '*Kinge Edward* sirnamed the longe, as fame telleth, made much of that rounde order of Knightes' and the creation of the Winchester Table is not the only example that we have of Edward's use of the iconography of the Arthurian tradition. The legends seemed to hold a particular attraction for Edward and it appears that he invested a great deal of time and energy in attempting to appropriate for himself some of the imperial grandeur of those long past times. As we have pointed out above, the historicity of Arthur was strongly supported during the Middle Ages in England and in these stories Edward seems to have seen a model for his own ambitions of conquest and rule across the British Isles. In the chapters that follow, we shall see that Edward throughout his reign made extensive and sustained use of the Arthurian legends for political and diplomatic purposes. After defeating the Welsh Prince Llywelyn ap Gruffydd for the first time in 1277, Edward attempted to authenticate his victory over this Celtic leader by appropriating the Celtic figure of Arthur as English. At Easter 1278 Edward visited Arthur's grave at Glastonbury, of which we shall read more in chapter 3, and in 1284 he had his son Alphonso present Arthur's Golden Crown for safekeeping in Westminster Abbey. These Arthurian objects were not simply used by Edward to demonstrate his domination of Wales and of the Welsh spirit, but their removal from Wales and transference to England was also part of the process of making the legends themselves English, rather than Welsh. The Round Table, the last of Edward's Arthurian constructions, seems to have been a further attempt to locate the Arthurian tradition and legacy within the heart of England and of the English – a process of cultural appropriation that has been more successful than Edward could have possibly imagined.

The Winchester Round Table, as it might have looked in 1290, seems to have been either unadorned or covered in cloth and used as a table rather than as a symbolic icon hung upon the walls of the great hall. John Hardyng, as we have seen, records in 1463-64 that the table 'hangeth yet' upon the wall, so we must assume that at some time during the 175-odd years between its construction and Hardyng's visit, the table's function and significance seems to have changed. To find the likely reasons that may lie behind this, we must move forward to the reign of Edward I's grandson, Edward III.

EDWARD III AND THE HANGING OF THE TABLE

The transformation of the table from a piece of furniture to a symbolic icon hanging upon the wall of the Great Hall is, in an important sense, the true moment of the creation of the Winchester Table. For it is as a relic of the Arthurian past that the Round Table has long been venerated. We have seen how Hardyng, Malory and Leland were all influenced by the immense presence of the relic, proudly displayed for all visitors to marvel upon. But how did the table make this transition from furniture to icon, and why? Who decided to hang it up and in what state was it displayed? We know from Hardyng's account that the table was hanging by 1464. This, however, is the only directly recorded observation of the table in the period between 1290 and Caxton's *Prologue* of 1485. In the absence of further contemporary accounts, we need to look again at the historical evidence in order to assess the possibilities.

This is in many ways the darkest and most murky period in the history of the table, as Winchester Castle fell out of royal use in the fourteenth century, due largely to the decreasing importance of Winchester as a city during the period. The situation was not helped by the devastating fire in the castle that occurred in 1302, resulting in the destruction of the royal apartments and effectively ending its role as a royal residence. Despite this, and fortunately for the Round Table, the Great Hall was maintained and was repaired on a number of occasions during the next 150 years: expense records survive for 1314, 1348-9, 1389 and 1425-8. While we cannot, of course, be certain, it is quite possible that the table would have been moved from the floor to the wall during one of these periods of renovation. The table could have been mounted upon the wall during any one of these events, or even at another unrecorded occasion, which leaves us little wiser as to when it may have happened.

We next must turn to the historical context of the table: were there any events that occurred during this period that may have been associated with the hanging of the table or perhaps any that may have brought back to the royal attention Edward's old wooden table that was languishing neglected in Winchester Castle? Professor Biddle has suggested that there was indeed such an event. In 1348, Edward III established in the Royal castle at Windsor the renowned, and still existing, Order of the Garter. This order of chivalry was almost certainly inspired by the Arthurian legends, as Edward III seems to have been, unlike his father Edward II, as passionately bewitched by the legends as his grandfather Edward I. The Order of the Garter seems, however, to have been Edward's second attempt to found such an organisation devoted to the tenets of knighthood. In 1344 he declared, so Adam Murimuth's *Continuatio chronicarum* tells us, that he would found in Windsor 'a Round Table in the same manner and form as the Lord Arthur, the once king of England, had done.' The rationale that lay behind Edward's desire to re-establish the Order of the Round Table is to be found in his love of the Arthurian legends. Jean le Bel tells us that Edward 'in the nobility of his heart resolved that he would rebuild the castle of Windsor, which Arthur first constructed and where the Round Table was first established, on account of the prowess of the knights who were there then, who had served him so well that he held them so worthy and noble that their peers would not be found in any kingdom: and it seemed to him that he could not honour them too much, so much did he love them.'

Although Edward seems never to have established such an explicitly Arthurian chivalric order, four years later he founded the Order of the Garter instead. Could there then perhaps have been some connection between Edward's vigorous interest in the Arthurian tradition and the hanging of the table? There certainly existed the kind of interest in the Arthurian tradition that would have lent itself to the hanging of the table, surely as some memorial to the Round Table and this in turn would have fed into the reputation of Winchester as an Arthurian site. Given the royal Arthurian hype of the surrounding years, if we are to identify one event during this period as likely to have witnessed the hanging of the table, then it is the renovations of 1348-9. It seems more than possible that Edward may have had the table mounted as a relic of

3 The emblem of Edward III's Order of the Garter, taken here from an alabaster tomb in Bath Abbey

the Arthurian past, given that he had founded the Order of the Garter in 1348. This point in the fourteenth century, more than any other, represents our best guess as to the date of the hanging of the table and represents another high point in the fluctuating tide of royal enthusiasm for the Arthurian past.

THE ORDER OF THE GARTER AND ARTHURIAN LITERATURE

The Order of the Garter, while not being explicitly Arthurian in its imagery, was clearly inspired by Edward III's love of the Arthurian legends. The ethos of Arthur's Round Table informs its conception and practices and provides the model for its international membership. Aside from these more obvious Arthurian associations, there also exists an intriguing connection between the Order and one of the greatest works of medieval English literature. In the fourteenth-century alliterative masterpiece *Sir Gawain and the Green Knight* we find a narrative that has curious links with the royal Arthurian enthusiasm of the period. This 2530-line Middle English poem tells the story of the giant-like Green Knight, who arrives one Christmas at Arthur's court and makes the following challenge: 'I shall let one of you here strike my head from my shoulders with my axe, on the condition that, in one year's time, you shall travel to my lands and allow me to return the blow.' This seemingly suicidal challenge is answered by Sir Gawain, the foremost of Arthur's knights in the English tradition. Having cleaved the giant's neck asunder, Gawain is then horrified to witness the giant raise himself to his feet, pick up his own severed head and proceed to remind Gawain of his obligation to meet him one year hence. One year later, honour-bound to fulfil his knightly oath, Gawain travels in search of the Green Knight. Near the climax of his journey he arrives in the castle of Hautdesert, where he passes the Christmas period with the castle's lord Bertilak. Here Gawain is once again challenged to a game of exchanges, this time of a seemingly trivial nature, when his host suggests that they exchange with each other whatever they should win over the next three days. Bertilak spends his three days hunting, while Gawain rests in his chamber. It is here where Gawain encounters the true test of his chivalric virtue, as

Bertilak's wife is intent upon seducing the glamorous knight from far off Camelot. After each of the first two days Gawain is forced to bestow on Bertilak what he has 'won', in his case kisses, in exchange for the fruits of Bertilak's hunting. On the third day, however, the lady offers Gawain a magical green girdle, or belt, which, she tells him, will save him from all harm. Seizing upon this possible solution to his imminent, and likely terminal, date with the Green Knight, Gawain accepts the lady's love-gift and withholds it from Bertilak in their last exchange. Gawain then departs for his tête-à-tête with his monstrous foe and meets him in a grim green chapel in the wilderness. The Green Knight twice swings the axe at Gawain's neck, rebuking him after he flinches on the first attempt, but withholding the killing blow. One the third blow he holds back once more and inflicts just a small cut on Gawain's neck. Gawain, having fulfilled his oath, leaps to his feet to face the giant, only to be met by the grinning Green Knight who reveals that he is in fact Bertilak de Hautdesert. It slowly dawns upon Gawain that his true test was not the beheading contest, but rather the test of his honesty and courtesy in the game of exchanges in the castle. Faced with his own culpability at breaking his self-declared code of honour, Gawain adopts the green girdle as a mark of his shame.

At the end of the poem, after Sir Gawain has returned from his marvellous quest bearing the green girdle, which is at once the sign of his moral failure and the symbol of his success in surviving the apparently suicidal quest, we find added to the manuscript the following motto: 'HONY SOYT QUI MAL PENCE'. Usually translated as 'Shame to him who thinks evil of it', the presence of the motto is significant in that it is a very slightly altered version of the motto of the Order of the Garter. It seems likely that the motto was added at a later date than the poem itself and thus the addition seems to be a comment by a later reader on the connections evident between Arthur's founding of the Order of the Green Girdle at the end of the poem and the Order of the Garter. While the Order of the Garter used a blue garter as their emblem, the parallels between the two orders would surely have been evident to the likely aristocratic audience of the poem. Whether the addition of the motto can be read as laudatory or critical of the Order of the Garter depends very much upon how one understands the highly ambiguous nature of the ending of *Sir Gawain and the Green Knight*

– whether the green girdle is to be understood as shameful or not – but which ever way one reads it we again see the use of Arthurian literature to comment upon the real-world practices of the fourteenth century. Leo Carruthers has suggested that the addition of the motto simply acts to make the implicit explicit, acting as one early reader's gloss upon the commentary that is already contained within the poem itself. This remains a difficult case to prove, but the possibility that the Gawain-poem is a critique of the honour of Edward's Order of the Garter is one that fits with what we know of the importance that was attributed to the Arthurian legends in fourteenth-century aristocratic culture.

THE LOOK OF THE THING

If we agree with Professor Biddle that there is every likelihood that the Round Table was hung on the wall of the Great Hall during the renovations of 1348-9 and there seems no strong reason to disagree with this hypothesis, then what might it have looked like? Prior to its hanging, we can only imagine that the table lay bare, stripped of the expensive cloth coverings that most likely adorned it during the 1290 tournament. Was it then hung up in this dilapidated state? Given what we know about the nature of medieval art and historical memorials, it is highly unlikely to have been displayed in such a condition. However, we also know that it was not painted in the manner in which it now appears as X-rays and paint analysis have demonstrated that it was not painted in its current design until the Tudor period. So, if the table was not painted, but was also unlikely to have been unadorned, then how might it have been identified for all to see as Arthur's table? Several points in Biddle's examination of the table have led him to suggest that the table may well have been covered with a decorated leather or cloth cover, which in turn may have been painted. This idea also makes sense if we consider the cultural purpose to which the table was being put. If those responsible for hanging the table had gone to such consider-able trouble to hoist the table onto the wall, and we must remember that it weighed around three-quarters of a ton, then it was obviously considered to be of some importance. Furthermore, once the table was on the wall, it would have made no sense to leave it unadorned – they would have wanted it to be readily identifiable to all that saw it as being Arthur's famous Round Table. In the absence of evidence of painting on the surface of the table itself, it would appear that any such identifying decoration must have been applied to some kind of attached cover. This decorative cover, whatever it may have been, was clearly Arthurian enough in nature for both Hardyng and Malory to identify it as being Arthur's Round Table – surely they would have less willing to make such claims had the table been but a bare wooden disk.

So what might this covering have been? From contemporary examples of other covered panels, doors and tables, it seems likely to have been covered in leather, secured by nails around the edges of the table. Wooden objects were often upholstered in leather, for reasons of appearance, preservation or comfort. The great size of the table would not have made such a covering unusual: we note that many church doors were also covered in leather during the medieval period, usually in cowhide, but occasionally reputed to be the skin of a marauding Dane. We also have some rare surviving examples of leather coverings that were used for murals and other paintings and it is this use that seems most likely for the covering of the Round Table. What, then, might have been painted upon the table's leather cover? Again we have no way of knowing for sure, but Biddle suggests two sensible possibilities. Firstly, there may have been a representation of the medieval Wheel of Fortune, an image that fits well with the shape of the table and is furthermore associated with Arthur through the tradition, passed down through the French *Mort Artu* to Malory, that Arthur had a prophetic dream featuring Fortuna's wheel the night before his final battle and death. This image has a noticeable affinity with the later Tudor painting of the table, that which is so familiar to us today, in that it would have had an image of Arthur himself at the top of the table, seated upon the wheel and about to begin his descent and fall. The second possibility that Biddle suggests, and in many ways this is the less problematic possibility, was that the covering was adorned with a design similar to that which was painted upon the table in the Tudor period. This is a tempting idea, as it fits well with the purpose and symbolism of the table itself and also goes some way to answering the question of where the painters of the table got their model for the table's modern appearance from. However, the design could not have been exactly the same, as a number of the Round Table's current design features are highly characteristic of Tudor iconography, including the Tudor red and white rose that lies at the central point of the table. Also different must have been the names of the knights, as some of these only entered the Arthurian tradition after Malory's *Morte Darthur* was written. However, despite these various possibilities, we do not know, and in all likelihood we will never know, exactly how the table was decorated at this point in its history. What we can be sure of is that it was during this period that Edward's I's feast-table became *the* Round Table and acquired its reputation as being an authentic relic of the Arthurian past – a reputation that influenced writers and kings alike. The hanging and decorating of the table seems to have transformed it from simply a piece of furniture, albeit a rather impressive one, into a cultural icon replete with Arthurian symbolism.

THE TUDORS AND THE ARTHURIAN AURA

When Henry Tudor, the Earl of Richmond, defeated Richard III at the battle of Bosworth Field in 1485, he lifted the crown from the blood-bespattered earth and thus began the reign of the Tudor Dynasty. Shakespeare, who faithfully reproduces so much Tudor mythology, captures the momentous effects that this battle had upon the history of England through the voice of Henry Tudor himself:

Proclaim a pardon to the soldiers fled
That in submission will return to us;
And then, as we have ta'en the sacrament,
We will unite the white rose and the red. (*Richard III*, V, 5, 16-19)

Shakespeare here reiterates one of the key tenets of the Tudor dynasty: their role in the healing of the rifts of the Wars of the Roses, the combining of the white and red roses, York and Lancaster and the healing of England. The Tudor Rose, both red and white, is the hybrid offspring of this union and became a central motif in Tudor iconography. At the centre of the Round Table we find painted just such a rose, pointing to the table's use as an item of some significant importance to the Tudor cause. Just why the Round Table takes on yet another political and cultural significance in the reigns of Henry VII and his son Henry VIII is entangled with the story of how the table took on its current iconic appearance.

While Henry Tudor, supported by what remained of the Lancastrian cause, had defeated Richard III and claimed the crown in battle, his claim by lineage to the throne was tenuous at best. Henry's claim was based upon his descent from one of the grandsons of John of Gaunt, the fourth son of Edward II. The strongest claimant at the time was in fact Elizabeth of York, Edward IV's daughter. Unsurprisingly, one of Henry's first acts to secure his rule was to promise to marry Elizabeth, thus ensuring that his children's right to the throne would become clear. The tenuous nature of the Tudor claim to the throne led to two major crises during Henry's reign, both of which were centred on pretenders who claimed to have stronger claims to the throne. The first of these involved one Lambert Simnel, who claimed to be Edward, Earl of Warwick, the nephew of Edward IV. Simnel, supported by mercenaries from Ireland and Germany, landed in England in 1487. However, his uprising lacked support and after being defeated by Henry at the Battle of Stoke in June 1487, he was captured. It seems that Henry saw Simnel as no real threat and, in an uncharacteristic demonstration of leniency, pardoned him and employed him as a servant in the royal kitchen. The second pretender to rise against Henry was Perkin Warbeck, who posed first as Edward, Earl of Warwick, just as Simnel had done, but then changed his story and claimed he was as Richard of York, Edward V's younger brother, who most thought had been murdered by Richard III in the Tower of London. Warbeck presented a more serious risk to the Tudor reign and raised considerable support from the continent, but after a number of incursions, he was eventually captured in 1497 and executed two years later. The shadow of usurpation lay heavy over the Tudor dynasty, allowing aspersions to be cast and rival claimants to be proposed and in an attempt to provide substance to their rule they looked towards their Welsh, and thus Arthurian, heritage.

That Henry saw the aura of the Arthurian tradition as useful to his reign is evident from his naming of his first son Arthur. Unfortunately for Henry and for the romance of English history, Arthur died young and it was his younger brother who went on to rule as Henry VIII. England's Arthurian heritage seems to have been of some use in terms of both national and international affairs during the early sixteenth century and it is within this sphere that we find a reminder of the importance of the Winchester Round Table. In 1506, Henry hosted Philip of Burgundy, King of Castile, at Windsor Castle. There they signed a treaty of friendship and King Philip was admitted to the Order of the Garter. After the ceremonies, Henry and Philip dined together at a round table. This table Henry afterwards compared to the Round Table at Winchester, promising that this table too would be hung upon the wall as a memorial of Philip's visit and would be decorated, just as the Winchester Table was, with the names of those who had dined that evening. This anecdote tells us two important facts about the Winchester Table. Firstly, that it must have been covered with some kind of decoration by 1506, most likely a decorated cover as we discussed above and secondly that the Round Table was considered by Henry as an object of sufficient importance to warrant acting as the model for the commemoration of such an august occasion. The importance of the Round Table in the Tudor resurgence of the popularity of the Arthurian myths is clear from the reference that Henry makes to it, demonstrating its high status as one of the relics of the Arthurian past. It was this renewed royal engagement with the Arthurian legends that seems to have led to the next stage of the transformation of the Round Table.

KING ARTHUR THE GREAT, I AM, I AM

The Arthurian legends were of great consequence to Henry VII and they, and the Winchester Table, seem to have had a similarly important role to play in the reign of his son Henry VIII. Over 24 and 25 June 1522, Henry VIII entertained Charles V, Emperor-elect of the Holy Roman Empire, in Winchester. This visit was part of an extensive series of pageants and visits that the two men had taken part in during Charles' visit of late May to early July of that year. At Winchester, Charles and Henry visited the Round Table which, as we have seen, had by this time become one of the most famous secular artefacts in England. Looking up at the table, Charles would have been particularly impressed, one can only imagine, at the image of Arthur himself at the top, an image that held a striking similarity with his host, Henry

VIII. Pamela Tudor-Craig, in her analysis of the painting of the table in Professor Biddle's study, has argued that it is likely that the painting of King Arthur on the table was intended to have just such a likeness to Henry and this is to be seen in both the shape of Arthur's face and in the cut of his beard. After all, who better to use as the model for how Arthur looked than his royal descendant (as the Tudors claimed). We might suspect that Henry may have had the Round Table painted especially for the visit of 1522, but the evidence suggests rather that it was more likely to have been done some six years earlier. Biddle has shown, once more using the royal financial accounts, that in 1516 the sum of £66 and 13 shillings was paid to one William Greme for the repair and renovation of the Great Hall and the Round Table. While the record of repairs to the table does not necessarily involve its painting, it is likely that any such repairs would have involved the removal of the decorated cover that had adorned it for so long. Once removed, it would seem unlikely that the table would have been left undecorated as a bare wooden disk, especially given the Tudor enthusiasm for the object. While 1516 looks like a probable date for the painting of the table, we can be certain that it had acquired its current appearance by 1522 – an appearance that had much to do with Henry's self-aggrandisement and his appeal to the power of the Arthurian legends.

The political currency of the legends was not limited to England alone. As we have seen, both Henry VIII and his father used the Round Table to impress their continental royal guests and the artefact seems to have been both well known and well regarded by these visitors. The European influence of the Arthurian stories has been well discussed, with versions of the legends appearing in almost all of the medieval European languages, from the major English, French and German works, through to Arthurian tales in Icelandic, Polish and even Hebrew. It is noteworthy that the guests who were taken to the Round Table during the early 1500s were both from the Hapsburg dynasty, a lineage that, significantly, also claimed a relationship with Arthur. The Hapsburgs were one of Europe's most powerful ruling dynasties and during the early sixteenth century, dominated the post of Holy Roman Emperor. The Emperor Maximilian, father of Philip of Burgundy and grandfather of Charles V, had as mother-in-law Margaret of York and it was through this link that he looked towards Arthur's imperial legacy. It is through the Hapsburg obsession with Arthur, Biddle suggests, that we can best understand the use that Henry VII and Henry VIII made of the Round Table. Perhaps we can see, in their repeated emphasis upon the table and upon the rest of England's Arthurian legacy, a statement aimed at the Hapsburgs to remind them that the aura of Arthur's glory lay firmly upon the kings of England and not upon their continental guests. Whatever the dynamics of this political and diplomatic interplay, we can see that the Arthurian legends, and the artefacts that they inspired, were considered to be of great importance. The political significance of the Round Table seems to have remained current while it was expedient for the English kings to keep the Hapsburgs on side. It is notable that after 1525, when Charles V captured the French King Francis I at the battle of Pavia, altering the long established balance of power in Europe and thus making an alliance with England much less of a priority, the usefulness of the Round Table diminishes immediately. We find no more examples of the use of Arthurian imagery in the relationship between England and the Hapsburgs after this date and the Round Table seems to be retired from active political use. Biddle notes that the Eternal Peace Treaty between England and France, signed in 1527, marks 'the end of the role of the Round Table in contemporary affairs. Henceforth, the table was an object of antiquarian interest not a political image.'

A MALLEABLE AND DURABLE SYMBOL

The Round Table would have appeared, by 1522, very much as it does today. Aside from a series of minor damaging incidents, including being used as a shooting target during the Civil War and the effects of occasional touch ups and other slight repairs in the intervening centuries, it has changed little. The table that so impressed John Leland in 1540 had completed its transformation from a thirteenth-century piece of furniture to the elaborately painted work of sixteenth-century century art that it is today. We have seen how, from its beginnings as an unpainted wooden table, perhaps adorned with cloth, it was slowly transfigured into *the* Round Table, hanging on the wall of Camelot as a relic of the imperial glory of Arthur's age. In the subsequent five centuries the Round Table has seen countless visitors, some finding in it confirmation of the truth of the Arthurian legends and others deriding it as mere superstition. Daniel Defoe, the very embodiment of the new educated student of history, comments in his *Tour of Britain* (1724):

> As to the Tale of King Arthur's Round Table, which, they pretend, was kept here for him, and his two Dozen of Knights; which Table hangs up still, as a Piece of Antiquity, to the tune of 1200 years, and has, as they pretend, the Names of the said Knights in Saxon Characters, and yet such as no man can read: All this Story I see so little ground to give the least credit to, that I look upon it, and't shall please you, to be no better than a FIBB.

While the medieval faith in the authenticity of the table largely disappears after the Tudor reign, the table remains a popular destination in its own right, speaking of a continuing fascination with both the object itself and the wider Arthurian tradition. The growing scepticism about both the table and the historicity of Arthur seems to have had little impact upon the symbolic importance that was attached to the table, culminating in its espousal as the symbol of National Association of Round Tables in 1929. This modern appropriation of an Arthurian symbol is very much in keeping with the variety of political and ideological uses to which the table has been put over the centuries. It is the very flexibility and malleability of the symbolic nature of the Round Table that has led to its longevity as an image and its adoption as the symbol of the Round Table movement speaks volumes about their commitment to the very Arthurian notions of common purpose, fellowship and community.

3

Hic Iacet Arthurus: memorials of the Arthurian past

In Glastenbury, Quia mirabilia fecit.

As one drives down the A39 from the cathedral city of Wells towards the Somerset town of Glastonbury, the road passes on the left a sign pointing to the rather romantically named Avalon Trading Estate. This road sign, which is often the first visual reminder of Glastonbury's Arthurian connections that meets the visitor arriving in the town, seems neatly to encapsulate the twin desires both to memorialise and to harness the popularity of the legends of Arthur and his knights. This inclination to commercialise the myth of Arthur can be readily experienced in its many manifestations simply by wandering through Glastonbury's many shops selling mystical crystals, replica crosses, plastic toy knights and books on every imaginable Arthurian theme. The more earnest visitor, we might imagine, abhorring what he or she considers to be the crass commercialisation of the modern age, turns away from such baubles and heads towards the serenity of the ruined abbey, or the windswept walk up to St Michael's on the Tor, seeking what they imagine is the true medieval Arthurian spirit of the place. However, what such visitors fail to realise is this: that the origins of Glastonbury's medieval Arthurian connections are deeply entwined with the very same commercial forces that they are fleeing, and in many ways the bustle of the tourist shops and the new-age boutiques are much more representative of the medieval attitude towards the usefulness of the town's Arthurian provenance.

Glastonbury has long attracted visitors to its historic town and abbey. In the medieval period Glastonbury Abbey was a major centre of Christian pilgrimage, attracting visitors who wished to see and touch its large collection of holy relics. However, it was not only the relics of the saints that pilgrims flocked to see, but also the grave, and later the tomb, of Arthur and the artefacts that the abbey claimed to have found therein. In this chapter we wish to explore the circumstances that surround the identification of Glastonbury as the site of Arthur's burial and the way in which the Arthurian connections of the abbey were subsequently developed and exploited by generations of monks in order to construct Glastonbury's reputation as the chief Arthurian location in England. As we shall see, the reasons that lie behind the discovery, or creation, of these relics has a great deal to do with both the popular attraction of the Arthurian legends and the political machinations of the English kings.

Burials, and the monuments that society creates to mark the places of the dead hold a particular attraction and fascination. These structures and places represent our link with the past – our connection with those who have gone before us – and are often sites of the commemoration of past victories and heroic deeds. This deep connection between memorials for the dead and the remembrance of the past is clearly visible today through the annual communal services that we hold at War Memorial monuments, our pilgrimages to the tombs of the famous and our own personal journeys to the gravesides of the loved and departed. Given the fascination with and deep reverence for the places of the dead that we observe in medieval culture, it would seem surprising if the location of King Arthur's burial was not memorialised during the Middle Ages. This, as it happens, is one of the most debated of aspects of the Arthurian legends: what did happen to Arthur, and if he did die, then where was he buried?

Geoffrey of Monmouth outlines the basic story of the fate of Arthur after he is wounded at the battle of Camlan:

4 The site of Arthur's black marble tomb at Glastonbury Abbey

Arthur himself, our renowned King, was mortally wounded and was carried off to the Isle of Avalon, so that his wounds might be attended to. He handed the crown of Britain over to his cousin Constantine, the son of Cador Duke of Cornwall: this in the year 542 after our Lord's incarnation.

Geoffrey later embellishes this sparse account in his *Life of Merlin*, providing further information as to the nature of Arthur's final destination:

The Isle of Apples [Avalon], which is also called the Blessed, has gained this name from its nature, since it produces all things spontaneously. It needs no farmers to till its soil: its only cultivation is that provided by nature. Untended, it bears rich crops, grapes and, in its woods, apples born of precious seed. Its soil freely produces everything like grass. The people on it live for a hundred years or more. Nine sisters rule there by right of birth over those who come to them from our lands. Their leader is more skilled at healing and more beautiful than her sisters. She is called Morgan, and has learned the properties each plant has to cure sick bodies. She also has the power of changing her shape, and of flying through the air on strange wings like Daedalus. She can be at Brest, Chartres or Pavia whenever she wishes, or glide from the sky onto our shores. She is also said to be learned in mathematics according to her sisters, Moronoe, Moroe, Gliorn, Glitonea, Gliten, Tythonoe, Tythen and Tithen, famed above all for playing the lyre. After the battle of Camlan we took the wounded Arthur to their island, led by Barinthus who was familiar with the sea and stars. With our ship under his direction, we arrived there with our leader and Morgan received us with due honour. She placed the king on golden coverlets in her bedchamber and herself exposed his wound with her noble hand. After examining it for a long while, she said that he might eventually recover his health, if he remained with her for a long time and was willing to submit to her care. So we joyfully entrusted the king to her and returned with a following wind in our sails.

Geoffrey here transmits the Celtic tradition that Arthur did not in fact die, but rather was carried off to some kind of Otherworld, an earthly paradise. The story of Arthur's withdrawal to Avalon serves to create a sense of lasting ambiguity as to his final fate and lies at the heart of the tradition that he would recover and lie in wait until his people needed him once more. This aspect of the legends appears in various forms: Arthur is said to remain in Avalon; to sleep in a cave under Snowdonia; or even to rule in the antipodes… The common factor in all these stories is a strongly held belief in his eventual return – a return that is often linked to a revival of the British nation.

For the English kings, the persistence of rumours of Arthur's return presented a continuing problem, in that it created a focus for rebellions and uprisings in the Celtic territories in which they wish to assert their control. The myth of Arthur's return features repeatedly in Welsh rebellions of the 1130s and even if the English did not themselves believe in such superstitious nonsense, they could clearly see that it had a significant unsettling effect upon their Welsh subjects. Faced with such a troublesome legend, surely the following thought must have crossed their minds: if only it could be demonstrated that Arthur was in fact dead, preferably in some highly visible and incontrovertible fashion.

THE DISCOVERY OF ARTHUR'S GRAVE

In 1191, the monks of Glastonbury Abbey made a discovery that, even by medieval standards, must have seemed incredible. In the very grounds of their abbey they had come across the long-lost grave of King Arthur himself. Gerald of Wales, in his *Speculum Ecclesiae* (*c*. 1215), relates the finding and exhumation of the grave:

> With immense difficulty, Arthur's body was eventually dug up in the churchyard dedicated by Saint Dunstan. It lay between two tall pyramids with inscriptions on them, which pyramids had been erected many years before in memory of Arthur. The body was reduced to dust, but it was lifted up into the fresh air from the depths of the grave and carried with the bones to a more seemly place of burial. In the same grave there was found a tress of woman's hair, blond and lovely to look at, plaited and coiled with consummate skill, and belonging, no doubt, to Arthur's wife, who was buried there with her husband.

The remains were raised from the grave and transferred by the monks to a magnificent tomb in the great church itself. Along with the two bodies, a vital piece of evidence was also found: a lead cross, engraved in ancient Latin characters, which declared that, 'Here lies buried the renowned King Arthur, with Guinevere his second wife, in the Isle of Avalon.' This relic of the Arthurian past, Arthur's own grave marker, proved to the monks that this was indeed the grave for which they had been searching. We will return to discuss the nature and significance of this Arthurian artefact shortly, but first let us consider the reasons that may have led to the Glastonbury monks' search and the implications that its discovery had for the politics of medieval England.

Just why the monks decided to search for the grave of Arthur has long been debated, but the chronicler Gerald of Wales gives us one near-contemporary view, attributing their explorations to the desires of King Henry II. Henry, Gerald tells us, had received secret information from a Welsh bard as to the location of the Arthur's final resting place:

> In our own lifetime, when Henry II was reigning in England, strenuous efforts were made in Glastonbury Abbey to locate what must have

once been the splendid tomb of Arthur. It was the King himself who put them on to this, and Abbot Henry, who was later elected Bishop of Worcester, gave them every encouragement ....The King had told the Abbot on a number of occasions that he had learnt from the historical accounts of the Britons and from their bards that Arthur had been buried in the churchyard there between two pyramids which had been erected subsequently, very deep in the ground for fear lest the Saxons, who had striven to occupy the whole island after his death, might ravage the dead body in their evil lust for vengeance.

Gerald seems to have had a great interest in the Arthurian legends, but was highly critical of many of the more outlandish tales told of Arthur's reign. Gerald's intended purpose in relating the story of the discovery of Arthur's body is made clear in his own work: he intended to correct what he saw as the superstitious beliefs of the ignorant peoples of the Celtic areas of Britain:

Many tales are told and many legends have been invented about King Arthur and his mysterious ending. In their stupidity the British people maintain that he is still alive. Now that the truth is known, I have taken the trouble to add a few more details in this present chapter. The fairy-tales have been snuffed out, and the true and indubitable facts are made known, so that what really happened must be made crystal clear to all and separated from the myths which have accumulated on the subject.

In making such criticisms of the Celtic belief in Arthur's return, Gerald was expressing his own strongly held view regarding the historical truth of Arthur. We must remember here that Gerald was in no way attacking the widespread belief in the historical verity of Arthur – he was far too traditional a medieval chronicler to do that – but was instead trying to correct what he viewed as a widespread historical fallacy. The version of Arthurian history that Gerald was promoting ran thus:

[After the battle of Camlan,] the body of Arthur, who had been mortally wounded, was carried off by a certain noble matron, called Morgan, who was his cousin, to the Isle of Avalon, which is now known as Glastonbury. Under Morgan's supervision the corpse was buried in the churchyard there. As a result, the credulous Britons and their bards invented the legend that a fantastic sorceress called Morgan had removed Arthur's body to the Isle of Avalon, so that she might cure his wounds there. According to them, once he has recovered from his wounds this strong and all-powerful King will return to rule over the Britons in the normal way. The result of all this is that they really expect him to come back, just as the Jews, led astray by even greater stupidity, misfortune and misplaced faith, really expect their Messiah to return.

Gerald's vehement contempt for the native Celtic belief in the hope of Arthur's return, here emphasised by his characteristically medieval anti-Semitic parallel, expresses his anxieties about the presence of competing historical narrative. For Gerald, the certainty of Arthur's death is not just a historical fact, rather it represents an ideological approach to how history should be evidenced and thus written. As the Winchester Round Table stood as manifest proof that Arthur had once lived, equally the discovery of Arthur's grave proved that he was now dead and gone. For Gerald, Arthur is history.

Henry II's interest in finding the grave of Arthur is a complex issue. We have only Gerald of Wales' account to tell us that Henry was behind the search and it is entirely possible that this was a story that was invented either by the Glastonbury monks, in order to place a royal seal of approval on their discovery, or even by Gerald himself. If, on the other hand, the record of Henry's interest is authentic, then we have to ask what benefit the king may have been seeking in encouraging the monks to find the grave. For Henry, had he survived to see the discovery, the benefits would have been two-fold. Firstly, as alluded to above, the discovery would have quashed the persistent rumours of Arthur's return, thus, so Henry hoped, greatly diminishing Arthur's use as a symbol of Celtic national feeling. Secondly, the prestige involved in being the custodian of such remains as those of the legendary Arthur would have aided Henry's cause both at home in Britain and on the continent. If, as we saw in the last chapter, the European kings and princes were impressed with the Round Table, then how much more impressed would they have been by Arthur's tomb and bones? Arthur, as a legendary king of England and an even wider European empire, would have acted as a symbol by which Henry could have glorified his identity as an English king of a British empire, in a similar fashion to the propaganda use that had been made of Charlemagne by the French Capetian kings.

LOCAL GRAVES FOR LOCAL PEOPLE

While Henry had clear political and cultural reasons for pursuing the location of Arthur's grave, one of the more intriguing things about Gerald of Wales' explanation of the reasons behind the monks' search is that it continues after Henry II's death. Henry died on 6 July 1189, yet despite the death of the king the monks continued with their search until the grave was discovered some two years later. This perhaps suggests that they were motivated by more than simply Henry's royal command, as the incentive for following most royal commands generally ended with the death of the king. One possibility is that the new king, Richard I, soon afterwards named as his heir his nephew Arthur, a fact that may well have spurred the monks onward in their search. However, Richard, as we shall see in chapter 4, had little regard for the Arthurian traditions of his English lands, a disdain that is best illustrated by his giving away a sword that was later claimed to have been Excalibur. Instead, there was a more immediate and local reason for the monks to discover the grave – money, or in their case a distinct lack of it.

In 1184 Glastonbury Abbey had suffered a devastating fire that damaged a large part of the abbey's buildings and destroyed many of the holy relics upon which much of the abbey's fame was founded. The monks, faced with a series of expensive structural repairs, were desperately short of money and must have wondered exactly how they were to manage. The money-raising plan that the monks decided upon seems likely to have had a major part in the discovery of Arthur's grave. An important source of income for monastic houses such as Glastonbury had always been the income brought in by visiting pilgrims and these pilgrims on the whole were attracted by a desire to see the holy relics of the saints. Therefore the quality and number of an institution's relics, in the context of the medieval pilgrimage industry, which was in many ways the equivalent of today's heritage tourist routes, had a direct correlation with visitor numbers. The loss of many of the abbey's relics represented a severe blow to both its prestige and its finances. When William of Malmesbury had visited Glastonbury in the early twelfth century, he recorded in his *De antiquitate Glastoniensis Ecclesie* (*Of the Antiquities of the Glastonbury Church*) that the abbey held relatively few notable relics, a list which stands in stark contrast to an updated list of the abbey's relics produced around 1230. In this updated list we find that the abbey has now, some 46 years after the fire, acquired a large number of new relics. The Glastonbury monks, in response to the destruction of their relics, seem to have fallen back upon hitherto unknown relics that they had secreted in and around the church. One such apparent discovery of forgotten relics was the finding of the bones of St Dunstan, which had been hidden away some 172 years beforehand. During the years following the fire, there seems to have been a concerted effort on behalf of the monastery to increase the number of holy relics that it held, presumably in an attempt to boost its prestige as a holy site and thus as a centre of pilgrimage. Seen in the context of the abbey's dire cash-flow problems, it is tempting to view the discovery of such an attention grabbing and potentially lucrative relic as the bones of King Arthur as being just the tonic that the abbey needed. The consensus amongst both historians and archaeologists today is that the discovery of the bones and the lead cross were part of an elaborate fraud perpetrated by the Glastonbury monks, in an attempt to help them recover from the precarious financial position in which the 1184 fire had left them. In this then, we can perhaps see the commercialisation of the Arthurian legends in modern Glastonbury as a strangely appropriate tribute to the medieval origins of Arthurian Glastonbury.

Was money the true motivation for the discovery of Arthur's grave? Most likely, although we can not of course be certain; however, regardless of the monks' original motivation, the event also lent itself to the political propaganda purposes that we have seen above and it was this political potential that brought the royal seal of approval to the discovery and subsequent memorialisation of Arthur's body.

WHY GLASTONBURY?

We have seen that the monks desired to have possession of the relics of Arthur for material reasons and seem to have concocted the whole story in order to provide a plausible backdrop to their claims. However, why were they so readily believed? What made Glastonbury such a convincing location for Arthur's grave? The answer lies in a tradition linking Arthur and Glastonbury, the origins of which can be found in the writings of a Welsh monk. Scholarly consensus holds that it was the *Vitae Gildae* (*Life of St Gildas*), written by Caradog of Llancarvan in the 1120s or 1130s, but most likely based upon a ninth-century original, that first established the Arthurian provenance of Glastonbury:

> Glastonbury was besieged by Arthur with a huge army because of his wife Gwenhwyfar, whom king Melwas had abducted and carried off to there, because of the invulnerable position's protection that was provided by the natural fortifications of rivers and marshes. Arthur had searched for the queen for an entire year, and at last he discovered that she was there. He then called up the armies of the whole of Devon and Cornwall and war was prepared between the enemies. When the abbot of Glastonbury, attended by the clergy and Gildas the Wise, saw this, he intervened between the contending armies, and advised king Melwas that he should restore the kidnapped lady. And so she was restored in peace and good will. When these things had been done, the two kings gave to the abbot many territories, and they came to visit the church of St Mary to pray.

One motivation that seems to have lain behind Caradog's account was an attempt to provide an origin story for the traditional wealth and privileges of the abbey. Such tales are commonplace in the *Vitae* of saints and were used to add the weight of history to the claims of a particular monastic house. In Caradog's case, his Glastonbury anecdote in the *Life of Gildas* had the added effect of establishing a lasting link between the abbey and Arthur. This link may well have been enough to suggest to the monks that there was a possibility that their claims would be believed. From this brief beginning, Glastonbury's Arthurian connections proliferated during the medieval period. The discovery of his grave was only the first such link that was made. During the next few hundred years Glastonbury became increasingly linked with Joseph of Arimathea and the Holy Grail, as well as with other Arthurian objects such as Craddok's mantle and the bones of Mordred.

THE GRAVE AND ARTHURIAN TRADITION

Although the 1191 discovery and exhumation of Arthur's body may seem like an obvious fraud to a modern reader of the events, the story seems to have been largely accepted by the chroniclers of the time and quickly became established as part of the Arthurian chronology. Gervase of Canterbury, writing in 1205, demonstrates the belief in this addition to the legend, as can be seen by the changes that he makes to it in writing his own *Chronicle of the Kings*. Taking his narrative from Geoffrey of Monmouth, Gervase follows his source faithfully except when it comes to the location of Arthur's burial, which he places firmly in the abbey at Glastonbury. From this first integration of the Glastonbury grave into the Arthurian legends, the event becomes a standard feature of many retellings of the myths. However, if the intention of the discovery of the grave had been to completely stamp out all stories of Arthur's possible return, then its success is questionable. Tales of Arthur as 'the sleeping king' continue to be told, especially in the Celtic regions of Britain, a fact that Malory integrates into his version of the death of Arthur. After Arthur has been wounded, he is carried by Sir Bedevere to the shore of the lake and then

> was he lad away in a shyp wherein were three quenys: that one was Kynge Arthur syster, Quene Morgan le Fay, the tother was the Quene of North Galis, and the thirde was the Quene of the Waste Londis. Also there was Dame Nynyve, the chyff lady of the laake ....

Bedevere, overcome with grief, wanders weeping through the woods all night. The next morning he arrives at a chapel, later identified as Glastonbury, which lies next to a hermitage. Inside this chapel he finds a hermit who is grovelling in tears next to a newly constructed tomb. The hermit tells Bedevere that, on the night before, a noble knight was brought here and buried by a number of mysterious ladies. Malory never explicitly tells us that this is Arthur's grave, but instead leaves it to Bedevere to make the obvious connection. Later, however, Malory tells of the uncertainty that still exists regarding Arthur's true fate:

> Yet som men say in many partys of Inglonde that Kynge Arthure ys nat dede, but had by the wyll of Oure Lorde Jesu into another place; and men say that he shall com agayne, and he shall wynne the holy Crosse. Yet I woll not say that hit shall be so; but rather I wolde sey, here in thys worlde he chaunged hys lyff. And many men say that there ys wrytten uppon the tumbe thys [vers]: HIC IACET ARTHURUS, REX QUONDAM, REXQUE FUTURUS.

Despite the persistence of such doubts about whether Arthur had in fact died, the 'discovery' of Arthur's grave had established Glastonbury firmly in the popular consciousness as the location of his grave. Furthermore, the exhumation had reinforced the abbey's reputation as an Arthurian site. Tom Shippey has argued that 'England has a kind of mythical geography, a network of associations and oppositions, now dwindled largely to humour and tourism, but once a vital part of the country's being: a geography which accords special roles to Oxford and Cambridge, to Stratford and Glastonbury, to Wigan and Jarrow.' Glastonbury's place within this 'mythical geography' has a great deal to do with its reputation as an Arthurian site, and the 1191 excavation can be seen to have played an important part in the construction of this reputation.

EDWARD AND ELEANOR: ARTHUR'S TOMB IN 1278

While the real reasons underlying the 1191 discovery of Arthur's grave may be clouded by the mists of time, the significance of the event was not lost on later generations of English rulers. Edward I, who as we have seen in the previous chapter was an enthusiastic devotee of the Arthurian legends, saw immediately the use of Arthur's grave in his conflicts with the Welsh. After his defeat of Llywelyn ap Gruffydd in 1277, Edward sought to demonstrate his domination of Wales and its rulers, and in what better manner to do this than to participate in a grand public ceremony designed to celebrate the fact that the great Welsh hero, Arthur, was truly dead and gone. For Edward, just like Henry II, had been greatly troubled by the Welsh rebels and their tiresomely unremitting hopes of Arthur's return. Edward's strategy of publicly demonstrating his conquest of Wales involved a number of such gestures, some of which will be discussed in chapter 5, but here we will examine his revivification of the importance of Arthur's tomb at Glastonbury.

At Easter 1278, Edward and Queen Eleanor made an ceremonious visit to Glastonbury Abbey, with the purpose of visiting Arthur's remains and witnessing their transfer from their old tomb to a magnificent new shrine in front of the high altar. On the evening of 19 April, Edward ordered that the old tomb should be opened and the contents removed. The next morning, with great pomp and ceremony, the remains were conveyed to their new resting place. Adam of Damerham records the event and highlights the important role played by both Edward and Eleanor in the ceremonies:

> King Edward again enclosed Arthur's bones in the chest, wrapped in a precious cloth, while Eleanor did the same for Guinevere's bones. They marked them with their royal seals and ordered the shrine to be put speedily before the high altar, while the skulls and the knee-joints were to be kept out for the devotion of the populace.

What is going on here is a clear secular parallel to what was known as the translation of a saint's bones. Holy relics were often moved from one location to another and when this was done the bones were usually treated with a great deal of respect and ceremony. In the translation of Arthur's bones from the old tomb to the new shrine, we see a similar degree of reverence and ritual. On the one hand this perhaps represents the exalted status that Arthur's relics had now obtained – to the monks of Glastonbury they rated amongst the most valuable of their crowd-drawing relics – but it also afforded Edward with just the type of formal ceremony that he desired to mark his defeat of the Welsh.

One significant aspect of the ceremony is the marking of the relics with the seals of Edward and Eleanor. What might this have been intended to mean to those watching the ceremony and to those who would later hear of it? Was Edward in some way literally and symbolically putting his mark on the Arthurian legends? This is a tempting way to understand Edward's actions and aligns well with his other uses of the aura of Arthur. For all those who would come to see the relics, it would now be impossible to deny their links with Edward. In one stroke, Edward had reminded his subjects both of Arthur's imperial authority, to which he was the rightful successor and to the fact of Arthur's undeniable death. Arthur was dead, you could see and touch his bones and, moreover, just as the body of the Welsh Prince Llywelyn would later do, they bore the tangible marks of Edward's power.

Like the Winchester Round Table, the shrine to which the relics were moved was another grand Edwardian construction. This new tomb, which Leland records as being of black marble, with two lions at each end and with an image of the king at the foot, sounds impressive indeed. Unsurprisingly, Edward seems to have spared little expense in constructing a grand memorial to Arthur. The position of the new tomb, which can be seen at Glastonbury today, was in front of the high altar, signifying its importance to the abbey and to the king: for what this new tomb represents is not simply a re-burial of Arthur's relics, but rather the transformation of those relics into a public, even a national, memorial. This memorialisation can be understood as an attempt to provide an official royal memorial to Arthur: a fitting tribute to a king who was becoming a central figure in the Arthurian rhetoric of Edward's imperial ambition.

ARTHURIAN RELICS: THE LEAD CROSS, CRADDOK'S MANTLE AND THE CRYSTAL CROSS

While Edward's tomb acted as the public focus for the remembrance of Arthur, the Arthurian relic that lies at the heart of the claims of the Glastonbury monks is the lead cross that Gerald claimed was discovered affixed to a stone slab under the grave. The lead cross was, both for the monks and for later chroniclers, the chief piece of evidence that proved that the grave was indeed the resting place of Arthur; after the exhumation it became a treasured relic of the monastery and was displayed in a position of prominence on the top of Arthur's black marble tomb.

We are fortunate to have a number of surviving descriptions of the cross, the best known of which is William Camden's illustration in the sixth edition of his *Brittania* (1607). While Arthur's tomb was destroyed during the ravages of the Reformation, his burial cross seems to have survived. John Leland claims to have handled the cross during his visits to the abbey and notes that it was around a foot in length. After the Reformation the cross seems to have stayed in ecclesiastical hands and it is last reported in the possession of one William Hughes, an official of Wells Cathedral, sometime in the early eighteenth century.

The nature and date of the lead cross have been the subject of much debate over the years, but it is now generally agreed that the cross should be seen as a product of the twelfth century and not earlier. The text on the cross – 'Here lies buried the renowned King Arthur, with Guinevere his second wife, in the Isle of Avalon' – is clearly derived from Geoffrey of Monmouth and we have evidence that there was a copy of Geoffrey's book present at Glastonbury from at least 1170. We will pass lightly over the debate regarding the date and various versions of the epitaph on the cross – there are fuller accounts of this argument to be read and it adds little to the question of the intended purpose of the object. It was long argued on epigraphic terms that the cross must have been of an early medieval date, given that the inscribed letters seemed to be characteristic of a period earlier than the twelfth century. However, the present consensus about the cross is that, while its lettering does appear somewhat old fashioned compared with other twelfth-century inscriptions, this should not necessarily place it outside of the monks' production. Given the high degree of sophistication and skill of monastic forgers in the medieval period, skills that are evident from the forged charters that are so common in this period, it seems unsurprisingly that the monks should have fabricated the cross in manner to give it an antiquated appearance. After all, this would merely add to the apparent authenticity of the fake relic.

The lead cross is perhaps the most famous Arthurian relic to have been associated with medieval Glastonbury and can today be purchased in a myriad of differing forms as a memento of one's visit to the abbey. But it was not the only Arthurian relic to become associated with the abbey. In one of the continuations of Chrétien de Troyes's Arthurian Grail romance, *Perceval*, we find the story of a magical mantle, or cloak, that was associated with a character called Craddok, or Caradoc. This virtue-testing cloak, which becomes a popular motif in variety of Arthurian tales, was reputed to have the magical ability to identify unfaithful wives. When placed upon the shoulders of such an immoral woman, the mantle would shrink, compressing her shoulders and marking her out for shame. In the versions of the narrative in which Craddok appears, his wife turns out to be the only faithful woman in the whole of Arthur's court.

As we highlighted in the introduction, Caxton informs us that Craddok's mantle could be seen at Dover beside Gawain's skull, as evidence of the truth of Arthur's existence. However, ownership of such valuable historical relics was rarely uncontested in the medieval period and Glastonbury too seems to have staked a claim to the mantle. Thomas Gray, an English knight who wrote the *Scalacronica* in the north of England in the fourteenth century, adapts Craddok's mantle story further: in Gray's version, Caradoc's (Craddok's) father arranges the test to prove the fidelity of his daughter-in-law, who passes the test of virtue with flying colours. At the end of the story, the mantle is presented to Glastonbury Abbey, where it is made into a chasuble. *The Short Metrical Chronicle*, found in the famous Auchinleck manuscript, also reports the presence of a fidelity-testing cloak belonging to 'Cradoc Craybonis sone' at Glastonbury. In this text the cloak is brought to Arthur's court in order to help reconcile Arthur and Lancelot, by testing the virtue of Guinevere, who has been hiding with Lancelot in the caves under Nottingham Castle. Although it seems that by Caxton's time Dover's claims to possession of the mantle had triumphed in the popular mind, the existence of the Glastonbury claims highlights once more the competition between various places for ownership of the Arthurian myths and possession of the relics that they engendered.

There is a further Arthurian relic associated with Glastonbury that deserves mention here. The heraldic arms of Glastonbury Abbey consist of a green shield, overlaid with a silver cross. In the top left-hand corner of the shield is an image of the Virgin Mary holding Jesus, while the other four corners contain crowns. In the late fourteenth century, the chronicler John of Glastonbury, a noted propagandist for the outlandish claims of the abbey, wrote a story explaining the origins of the abbey's arms. Arthur, so John relates, was staying one night in the nunnery of

St Peter's on Wearyall Hill. While sleeping in his carved bed, Arthur received a visitation from an angel, who told him that he must go to the hermitage at Beckery, nearby in the fens. Sir Gawain, who was worried as to the implications and origins of the dream, advised him against this, but the angel returned the next night. On the third night Arthur's squire dreamed he had visited the chapel, seen a dead body, stolen a golden candlestick and had been wounded. On waking the squire discovered that he was indeed mortally wounded and revealed the candlestick before bleeding to death. Arthur, somewhat taken aback by this turn of events, decided to visit the hermitage after all. Arriving at the hermitage, the king found it guarded by two strange disembodied hands, each wielding a sword. Inside the chapel he encountered a priest and witnessed a miraculous manifestation of the miracle of transubstantiation. In the presence of the Virgin Mary, Arthur watched as she offered up her son, in place of the host, as a sacrifice at the mass. Once this miracle had been competed, the Virgin Mary offered to Arthur a cross made of crystal. Arthur hence adopted the image of the cross, with a figure of Mary and her Child, in silver on a green ground, as his coat of arms and it was later adopted by Glastonbury Abbey.

This episode, which attaches to Glastonbury a story found in the anonymous *Perlesvaus*, has two important consequences. Firstly, it creates an origin story to explain where the abbey's coat of arms comes from, and secondly it provides the monks with yet another set of Arthurian relics. The crystal cross was kept under guard in the abbey and the candlestick was deposited in the royal treasury at Westminster which, as we shall see in the next two chapters, is another common destination for Arthurian relics. Both relics are now lost, but the cross was for many years revered as a significant item amongst the abbey's treasures. We might view John's tale of the origins of the crystal cross as the literary equivalent of the 1191 discovery of Arthur's bones. The tale allows the creation and authentication of a new relic, which would have added to the abbey's prestige. Such was the power of written authority in the medieval period that the real in many ways seems to manifest from books. In the same way that the stories of the Round Table led to its construction, John's tale most likely created the relic of the crystal cross.

IN SEARCH OF GAWAIN

While the Glastonbury grave was the most famous Arthurian burial site, the remains of other prominent knights were also identified. Caxton identifies Gawain's skull as lying in Dover Castle, where in his day it could still be seen. However, much like Craddok's mantle, Dover's claims were not uncontested. When Gawain is killed in Geoffrey's *History*, the reader is given very little specific information: 'In the battle which ensued Mordred inflicted great slaughter on those who were trying to land. Auguselus, the king of Albany and Gawain, the king's nephew, died that day, together with many others too numerous too describe.' Wace adds the detail that the king lamented Gawain's death, while Layamon lets Gawain kill a Saxon leader's son before an earl kills him. Gradually, more and more detail is added from text to text. Gray includes another detail of interest to readers of Malory: like Malory, Gray insists that Gawain was buried at Dover, where both Caxton and Raimon de Perillos would later claim to see his skull and where the French romances had placed his last, fateful battle with Mordred.

However, Geoffrey of Monmouth's failure to specify a site for Gawain's last battle created another example of fecund ambiguity and meant that Dover would not be universally accepted as Gawain's final resting place. In the early twelfth century, William of Malmesbury had reported an earlier tradition that situated Gawain's grave in Wales.

> At that time in the province of Wales, called Ros, was found the sepulchre of Walwin [Gawain], the noble nephew of Arthur; he reigned, a most renowned knight, in the part of Britain which is still named Walwerth; but was driven from his kingdom by the brother and nephew of Hengist … though not without first making them pay dearly for his expulsion. He deservedly shared, with his uncle [Arthur], the praise of retarding, for many years the calamity of his falling country. The sepulchre of Arthur is nowhere to be seen, whence ancient ballads fable that he is still to come. But the tomb of the other [Gawain], as I have suggested, was found in the time of King William, on the seacoast, fourteen feet long; there, as some relate, he was wounded by his enemies, and suffered shipwreck; others say, he was killed by his subjects at a public entertainment. The truth consequentially is doubtful.

William records one of the various stories regarding the resting place of Gawain and interestingly compares the tale with the lack of any concrete site for Arthur's burial. The discovery of Gawain's grave in the reign of King William II (1087-1100) does not seem to have had the same kind of lasting effect as the discovery of Arthur's grave, and this is most likely due to the lack of an institution, such as Glastonbury Abbey, who might have had a vested interest in maintaining and promoting the claims.

While the Welsh may have claimed Gawain as their own, there also existed a strong tradition linking him with Scotland. A minor Arthurian text, known simply as *Arthur* and contained in a manuscript dated to 1428, insists that Gawain is buried in his Scottish homeland:

Gawain's body, as I'll explain,
And other lords that were dead,
Arthur sent into Scotland,
And buried them there, I believe.

The 'other lords' surely refer to, among others, Anguselus, the Scottish king who died in the same battle as Gawain in Geoffrey and some of his followers. Gawain alone is specifically sent to Scotland for burial, implying that by the fifteenth century he was beginning to be seen as Scottish rather than English. Malory confirms this when Gawain's brothers, Agravain and Mordred, attempt to trap Lancelot in the queen's bedchambers and expose the long affair:

Than Sir Aggravayne and Sir Mordred gate to them twelve knyghtes and hyd hemselff in a chambir in the castell of Carlyle – and thes were their namys: Sir Collgrevaunce, Sir Mador de la Porte, Sir Gyngalyne, Sir Mellyot de Logres, Sir Petipace of Wynchylsé, Sir Galleron of Galoway, Sir Melyon de la Mountayne, Sir Ascamore, Sir Gromore Somer Joure, Sir Curselayne, Sir Florence, and Sir Lovell. So thes twelve knyghtes were with Sir Mordred and Sir Aggravayne – and all they wereof Scotlonde, other ellis of Sir Gawaynes kynne, other well-wyllers to hys brothir.

Clearly then, in Malory, Gawain's connections are Scottish. His father's kingdom, Lothian, also comes to include the Orkneys and in the ebb and flow of medieval politics Lothian, once part of English territory and later a border region, becomes a part of Scotland. T.H. White, following Malory for his twentieth-century Arthurian quartet *The Once and Future King*, gives Gawain a noticeable Scottish brogue.

Scottish or not, Gawain's death is an integral part of the tragedy of Arthur's fall, but Geoffrey's failure to provide specific details meant that later authors would attempt to fill in the blanks. The author of the *Didot-Perceval* (*c.*1210) adds a detail that echoes throughout the Arthurian tradition when he describes how Gawain, burning with shame at Mordred's treachery, storms the English beach without remembering to lace his helmet. Gawain's characteristic rage undoes him here, as a flailing Saxon oar blow to the head kills him instantly. Following this story, Gawain's death-wound becomes established as a head wound: in Gray's *Scalacronica*, which is derived from the *Brut* tradition and does not include Lancelot, when Gawain is injured during the Roman War the injury is still a head wound. Head wounds were not always fatal during the Middle Ages, but they were understandably taken seriously. In a celebrated historical case, Lazzarino of Cremona received a serious sword wound to the head. The attending physician, Guglielmo, declared that Lazzarino would probably die. The patient soon became 'paralyzed and incontinent' but with 'the healing power of nature and Guglielmo's treatment, however, he ultimately recovered completely and lived another 20 years'. Head injuries were generally, as we might expect, extremely serious and Guglielmo was an extraordinarily cunning doctor with a superlative reputation. When a medieval author decides that Gawain's death is the result of a head wound, he wants to be certain the reader knows the seriousness of the injury.

The *Alliterative Morte Arthure* is alone in having Mordred kill Gawain, but here too the wound is to the head, 'with a trenchand knife the traitour him hittes / Through the helm and the hed on high the brain.' The *Stanzaic Morte Arthur* agrees with the narrative found in the *Didot-Perceval*:

Sir Gawain armed him in that stound;
Alas! Too long his hede was bare;

He was seke and sore unsound;
His woundes greved him full sore.
One hit him upon the olde wound
With a tronchon of an ore;
There is good Gawain gone to ground,
That speche spake he never more.

One can begin, perhaps, to see a pattern linking a text's attitude to
Gawain with the manner of his death. Malory's two major sources for
the last book, the *Mort Artu* and the *Stanzaic Morte Arthur*, both agree
that Lancelot gives Gawain his death wound: even if in both cases
Lancelot's responsibility is once removed. Malory furthermore tells us
that in his own time 'all men might see his [Gawain's] skull and the same
wound can be seen that Sir Lancelot gave him in battle'.

The presence of Gawain's skull at Dover, a site traditionally associated, for obvious reasons, with the defence of the British coast, reminds
us of the peculiar Welsh legend of Brân the Blessed's head. Brân (in
Welsh, Bendigeidfran) appears in the *Mabonogi* of Branwen Daughter
of Llyr, his sister, where he commands his followers to behead him and
bury the head (which is still said to 'be as pleasant company as ever it
was at best when it was on me') on the White Mount in London, facing
France and the continent. This White Mount is now the location of
the White Tower (another monument that was reputed in the medieval
period to have been built by Arthur), where ravens are still kept with
their wings clipped to prevent their departure, which legend tells would
herald the ruin of Britain. Similarly, the burying of Brân's head was said
in the Welsh Triads to be 'one of the Three Happy Concealments … for
no plague would ever come across the sea to this Island so long as the
head was in that concealment'. Unfortunately, a later Welsh legend tells
us that the head was eventually unearthed as 'one of the Three Unhappy
Disclosures', sealing Britain's fate, and the man who uncovered Brân's
head was none other than Arthur: 'because it did not seem right to him
that this Island should be defended by the strength of anyone, but by
his own'. Perhaps Gawain's skull, facing across the Channel where he
met his death, on some level reverses Arthur's proud mistake: the dead
Gawain is forever more at the on the shores of Britain, glaring across
at the continent.

THE POWER OF THE DEAD

The relics of the Arthurian past held great influence in the Middle Ages and were viewed as providing a direct link to the glories of those long dead and gone. We have seen how relics such as the bones and tomb of Arthur, the Glastonbury lead cross, the crystal cross of Beckery and the skull of Gawain were used for a variety of different reasons: to enhance the prestige of a particular ecclesiastical house, to raise funds by attracting pilgrims and for the purposes of political and nationalist propaganda. Both Henry II and Edward I seem to have been worried by the existence of Celtic stories that prophesised the return of Arthur, which appear to have been believed by the Celts with an almost messianic fervour. The reality of the Celtic threat in the twelfth century should not be underestimated: by the time of Henry II it seems that something needed to be done to quash the recurrent rumours of Arthur's return, which had been used on a number of occasions as a rallying call in Welsh rebellions. It is perhaps in the context of the usefulness of the 'once and future' nature of Arthur that we can best understand the political motivations that may have lain behind the royal encouragement of the Glastonbury monks in their 'discovery' of Arthur's grave: for if Arthur's body was to be found and his remains displayed for all to see, then the Welsh could hardly continue to claim that he did not die. In addition, the identifying of Arthur's grave in the heart of one of England's most powerful and venerable monasteries located the legendary king very much outside of the Celtic territories, and appropriated Arthur once and for all for England.

4
Of arms and the king

One of the things a modern reader is most likely to know about the Arthurian legends is the fate of Arthur's sword Excalibur, that wondrous blade given to him by the Lady of the Lake. Originally called Caliburn by Geoffrey of Monmouth, Arthur's sword is inextricably linked with the legendary monarch, so much so that the sword must disappear when Arthur passes from this life into the next. In French Arthurian legend, the mortally wounded Arthur asks his sole surviving knight, Sir Griflet, to throw Excalibur into a nearby pool of water that is similar to the pool from which the sword originally came. In Malory's English retelling, the role that Griflet plays is transferred to Sir Bedevere:

> Than sir Bedwere departed and wente to the swerde and lyghtly toke hit up, and so he wente unto the watirs syde. And there he bounde the gyrdyll aboute the hyltis, and threw the swerde as farre into the watir as he myght. And there cam an arme and a honde above the watir, and toke hit and cleyght hit, and shoke hit thryse and braundysshed, and vanysshed with the swerde into the watir.

Bedevere's disposal of the sword would imply that, above all other Arthurian relics, Excalibur would remain forever lost, and by the express wishes of the king at that. As we shall see, this was not to be the case and the desire of later chroniclers and kings to lay claim to the fabled weapon testifies to its importance as a symbolic relic of the Arthurian past.

Despite its matchless fame, Excalibur was not the only famous sword associated with Arthur and his knights. By their very nature, each of the Round Table's champions possessed weapons which might conceivably survive the passage of time. Caxton tells us that it was still possible, in 1485, to see Lancelot's sword, although he is very vague about where one might find the great knight's blade: perhaps he had in mind Alnwick or Bamborough, which Malory claims are the leading candidates for Lancelot's English stronghold, Joyous Garde. The sword of Tristram was once said to be included in the regalia of King John (*c.*1207) and has from time to time been identified with Curtana, the sword without a point carried in English coronation ceremonies.

Arthur himself was associated with a variety of swords in medieval tradition. In the Welsh *Dream of Rhonabwy*, Arthur's unnamed sword, guarded by his cousin Cador of Cornwall, is described as having two serpents etched in gold on the blade, which seemed to breath fire when the blade was drawn from its sheath: difficult, some might think, for modern memorabilia companies to recreate for Arthurian enthusiasts. The chronicle tradition descended from Geoffrey of Monmouth maintained the king's association with Excalibur or Caliburn, with one chronicler, Robert of Gloucester, almost seeming to knight the sword as if it were a person:

> Sir Caliburn, his sword, he [Arthur] began to shake anon.
> And slew to the ground here and there, but he never smote anyone
> Without slaying both him and his horse; amongst all of these
> Was the king of Libya and Bithynia, who he himself killed
> With Caliburn, sending his heathen soul to hell.

For Robert of Gloucester, Arthur and his sword are almost indistinguishable, man and weapon united in the effort of defending the Christian faith and safeguarding the kingdom of the Britons.

Medieval Arthurian romance, however, identifies three swords which are said to have strong connections with Arthur: [1] the sword from the stone; [2] the sword given to Arthur by the Lady of the Lake (these two seem to have been conflated in the later Arthurian tradition); and [3] a sword called Marmiadoise which once belonged to Arthur's early enemy, King Ryons, a collector of royal beards and a descendant of Hercules. Marmiadoise has further mythic associations: this sword is said to have been forged by the Roman smith-god Vulcan and comes to be associated with the violent history of Thebes, noted in the Middle Ages for its connection with incest, through Oedipus and fratricide, through his sons Eteocles and Polynikes. This attempt to link ancient Greek mythology with the Arthurian legend appealed to a medieval interest in the circular nature of world history: authors and readers could find parallels between the violent stories of heroes no matter how distant they were from each other chronologically. The same book further implies that the name Excalibur, which meant 'cuts iron and steel and wood' in French, was in origin a Hebrew word. Although we are not told what the name might mean in Hebrew, the implication that Excalibur has a role to play in God's plan for the world is inescapable. In one French text, Arthur is said to greatly prefer Marmiadoise to any other sword, which perhaps implies a rejection of the spiritual in favour of the legendary heroic past. In any event, even before the death of King Ryons, Arthur gives Excalibur to his nephew Gawain, so that the younger man can act as Arthur's surrogate in tournament and adventure. Modern interpretations of the legend that emphasise the symbiotic nature of Arthur's relationship with Excalibur (for example, in John Boorman's film *Excalibur*) are privileging a dependence on the blade that the medieval king does not seem to acknowledge.

Arthur's association with Marmiadoise reminds us that Excalibur is only one of many famous swords in medieval legend, some of which were beginning to reappear (or perhaps 'be recycled' is a better term) in the later Middle Ages. The Middle English poem *Guy of Warwick* tells the story of Guy's battle with a Saracen champion, Amoraunt, who wields the sword that once belonged to the Trojan Prince Hector. The explicit connection here between the sword and Hector suggests, to the alert medieval reader, an intriguing link with another famous medieval literary sword. In the *Song of Roland*, the eponymous hero's blade is also claimed to have once belonged to Hector. This sword is the mighty Durendal. After Roland's lamentable death at Roncevalles, Durendal falls into the hands of the heathen Saracens and Guy's subsequent claiming of the sword seems to complete the sword's journey from worthy pre-Christian pagan to Christian champion, to heathen enemy and finally back to a Christian knight. As with Marmiadoise, the story of Hector's sword links the distant past with more recent legendary history. In common with many of the Arthurian relics mentioned by Caxton, Guy's sword and armour were preserved, in this case in the treasury of Warwick Castle and became valuable heirlooms of the Earls of Warwick, kept under the protection of a custodian appointed by royal patent.

In a similar vein, Attila the Hun claimed a sword that had been sacred to the Scythians of the Asian steppes and was further associated with the Roman god of war Mars. Attila had received this fearsome weapon from a herdsman, who had found it stuck in the ground as if it had fallen from the sky. It was believed that Attila had been given dominion over the known world along with the sword. Attila's sword was said to have survived; in 1063, it came into the possession of Liutpold of Meersburg, an ally of the Holy Roman Emperor Henry IV in his battle against a new invasion from the steppes, one of many during the Middle Ages. During the campaign, Liutpold fell from his horse and landed on the sword, managing to fatally injure himself in the process. This event was recorded by the chronicler Lampert of Hersfeld, who interpreted the event as demonstrating that the sword's association with Attila's pagan attack on Christian Rome made it a blade unfit for a Christian knight to wield. Attila's sword remained fundamentally anti-Christian, but despite this reputation, claimants to the Hungarian throne still tried to bolster their chances by claiming possession of the fabled weapon.

Even less celebrated swords could play a political role, representing the interests of their owners and symbolising the land that the sword itself had won. John de Warrene made such symbolic use of a sword in resisting the statute *Quo Warranto* ('Who Holds?'), which demanded written proof of the titles held by various noble families. Earl de Warrene appeared before Edward I brandishing a rusting blade of great antiquity, snarling that he held the very sword which had won his lands during the Norman Conquest and that he needed no other documentation to prove his claim. The sword itself was the claim and the proof. In a similar example of the link between venerable swords and the owner-ship of land, the aristocracy of County Durham traditionally met the Prince-Bishop of Durham at Neasham Ford (also called Sockburn) to present him with the Conyers Falchion, another ancient weapon. The

Conyers Falchion was reputed to have been used by Sir John Conyers to slay a dragon in the years before the Normans came; this story obviously has no basis in truth, but the ritual itself represented the essential political and social links between the powerful bishops of Durham and the local nobility which served their interests. If swords such as those of Atilla or the Conyers Falchion were considered valuable as political relics, then how much more tempting might it have been to English monarchs to make use of Excalibur?

Malory tells us that Arthur loses Excalibur on at least one occasion, along with its magical scabbard, which Merlin pronounces of greater value than the sword, for it protects the wearer from incurring any loss of blood. Early in Malory's story, Arthur gives the sword and the scabbard to his half-sister, Morgan le Fay, for safekeeping; at this point in the narrative she has not yet revealed herself as his enemy. Treacherously, Morgan has copies made and gives the real items to her lover, Accalon of Gaul, before manipulating both brother and lover into a duel:

> And so they went egerly to batayle and gaff many grete strokes. But allwayes Arthurs swerde bote [bit, or cut] nat lyke Accalons swerde, and for the moste party every stroke that Accalon gaf he wounded sir Arthure sore, that hit was mervayle he stood, and allwayes his blood felle frome hym faste. Whan Arthure behelde the grounde so sore bebledde [blood-spattered] he was dismayde. And than he demed [knew that it was] treson, that his swerde was chonged, for his swerde bote nat steele as hit was wonte to do. Therefore he dred hym sore to be dede, for ever hym semyd that the swerde in Accalons honde was Excaliber, for at every stroke that Accalon stroke he drewe bloode on Arthure.

Only the timely intervention of Nimuë, the Damsel of the Lake, saves Arthur from certain death. She causes Accalon to drop Excalibur and Arthur quickly retrieves the weapon, chiding the sword as he does so: "'A,' seyde Arthure, "thou haste bene frome me all too longe and muche damage hast thou done me!"' The relationship between Arthur and Excalibur is a curious one, and we begin to see where Boorman and others derive the inextricable link between Arthur and Excalibur. It is clear that Morgan arranges her treachery for the purpose of putting

Accalon on the throne of England, as Accalon confesses as he lies dying at the end of the battle. Possession of Excalibur is, it seems here, an important factor in the possession of the kingdom. Given the connection between Arthurian symbols and kingship that we shall see in the next chapter, it would be intriguing to discover how Excalibur was put to political use in the Middle Ages. However, as we shall soon see, when it does appear it is in somewhat surprising circumstances.

THE LION-HEART IN SICILY

In 1190, while en route to the Holy Land for the Third Crusade, Richard the Lion-hearted became embroiled in a dispute with King Tancred of Sicily, another kingdom that – like England – had been conquered by the enterprising Normans. Tancred was a usurper who had seized power following the death of William II (called 'the Good') and who had only recently managed to quell both a rebellion led by his rival Roger of Andria and an insurrection amongst the island's substantial Muslim population. It is during Richard's visit to the island that we find the first example of Excalibur being used as a political tool, an important and valuable symbolic item in a game of royal one-upmanship played out amongst Richard, Tancred and Richard's erstwhile political ally and personal rival King Philip Augustus of France.

Tancred's predecessor, William the Good, had been married to Richard's sister Joanna and he had promised Richard's father Henry II gold and supplies if he ever went on crusade: a promise that Richard fully intended to collect in his father's place. Tancred, on the other hand, seems to have had little intention of honouring a promise made by one dead king to another equally dead king. To further inflame this volatile situation, Tancred had made Joanna a virtual prisoner following the usurpation: she was simply too dangerous to Tancred's interests and could not be allowed to roam the island freely in case she became a rallying point for further rebellion. The imprisonment of his sister, and perhaps more importantly the withholding of the promised supplies, were more than adequate as excuses for an ambitious monarch looking for a bit of adventure and profit.

Richard's arrival had one immediate result: Joanna was given her liberty and a large sum of money for her troubles. Richard, however, was nothing if not persistent in the pursuit of what he saw as his rights. He immediately occupied Bagnara, a small town, and a monastery dedicated to Christ the Saviour in Messina, the Sicilian capital. Using the monastery as a base for his army, he proceeded to loot Messina, despite the diplomatic efforts of the French king Philip Augustus. Tancred, in residence in southern Sicily at Catania, reacted to the assault with alarm. He made three attempts to placate Richard's wrath before succeeding in quelling the dispute. On 3 March 1191, Richard and Tancred met at Catania and exchanged gifts to seal their peace; Richard insisted on accepting only a small ring from Tancred, but in return he gave the Sicilian king Excalibur, sword of Arthur, king of the Britons.

Roger Howden tells the story, basing his account on that of Benedict, abbot of Peterborough Abbey:

On the fourth day the king of Sicily sent to the king of England many presents of great value, consisting of gold and silver, horses and silken cloths; but he would receive nothing from him except a little ring, which he accepted as a token of their mutual esteem. On the other hand, the king of England gave to king Tancred that most excellent sword which the Britons call 'Caliburn,' and which had been the sword of Arthur, once the valiant king of England.

Richard's generosity seems astounding, especially after such a forceful display of aggression in Messina. However, while Roger's account concentrates upon the central importance of the exchange of gifts, he further tells us, almost in an aside, that 'King Tancred also gave to the king of England four large ships, which they call "ursers" and fifteen gallies.' While these additional gifts are, in a symbolic sense, of much less importance that the ring and the sword, they do alter markedly our understanding of the transaction; a small Sicilian armada would not be unhelpful in Richard's proposed re-conquest of the Holy Land. This story of Richard's munificence proved to be a popular one, becoming part of the medieval reputation of Richard and later being retold by Brother Walter of Coventry in his *Memoriale* and by Thomas Gray in the *Scalacronica*.

Roger's reluctance to mention the extent of the transaction between Richard and Tancred is more than simple avoidance of unchivalric economic issues, nor is it only a desire to avoid the success of Richard's martial blackmail techniques. There is a strong sense that Richard is shaming Tancred by giving the latter a far better gift than he himself is receiving; the ancient and nearly universal gift-giving rituals sometimes known to anthropologists as the pot-latch (named after the practice of the North American Nootka people) are entirely predicated on the ability of aristocrats to compete with one another in ostentatious generosity. Richard accepts a small, almost insignificant ring and leaves behind an ancient relic of great symbolic power. We need not be distracted by Richard's lack of sentimentality concerning the treasures and relics of his own English kingdom, as he may once have famously offered to sell London in order to raise funds for a crusade, if only he could find a buyer. More importantly, Richard was a consummate showman, and, in the case of Norman Sicily, he knew his audience.

Richard's arrival in Sicily on 23 September 1190, nine days after that of his rival Philip Augustus, was testimony to his mastery of pomp and pageantry. According to the *Itinerary of Richard I*, the inhabitants of Messina had been terribly disappointed by Philip's low-key arrival; the French king had arrived on a single ship and with a minimum of fuss. The people of Messina 'saw this as a sign of weakness; such a man, they said, was not likely to be a performer of any great matter.' Richard, on the other hand, arrived accompanied by a number of galleys, each arrayed with pennants and the sound of trumpets. Richard was described as 'loftier and more splendid than all his train' and certainly more impressive than the French king. It would seem churlish to mention, then, that his sea-voyage had been quite short, only a few miles from the Italian mainland. The Lion-heart had wisely marched his army down the peninsula because he was afraid of seasickness. For Richard, the show was the thing, not the reality.

Richard knew that he could count on a Sicilian, and a wider Italian, knowledge of the Arthurian legend. Not only was Geoffrey's *History* making the rounds throughout Europe and especially Norman Europe, but the Sicilian Mount Etna was said to be one of Arthur's many resting places. In Italy itself, one of the earliest testaments to the medieval interest in Arthur was to be found in Modena, above the cathedral doors, where a sculpture now dated prior to Geoffrey's book depicted the rescue of Guinevere by Arthur of Britain, Gawain, Kay and others. Arthurian names (including Arthur itself and Gawain) begin to appear in northern Italy from the same period. Still, mere knowledge of Arthurian legend does not provide an entirely satisfactory explanation for Richard's gift and it has been queried whether Tancred could really have fully appreciated the gesture. In addition, we might instead wonder why Richard did not appreciate Excalibur a little more, his opinion of London notwithstanding. The answer, it seems, is to be found within the wider question of just how Excalibur came into Richard's possession in the first place.

Pierre de Langtoft, writing during the later reign of Edward I, wrote that the sword had been found during the exhumations at Glastonbury, lying beside Arthur's body (presumably on the other side from Guinevere). Contemporary accounts from Glastonbury, however, do not mention a sword. Even if we accepted that Excalibur had been found, or manufactured, during the excavations at Glastonbury, John Julius Norwich is surely right to note that the weapon 'would have needed all of its magical properties to reach Sicily by early March', given that the exhumation had taken place only a short time earlier. Langtoft's theory is clearly an attempt to explain Roger Howden's claim, preferably while further developing his own interest in the Arthurian heritage of his patron Edward I. The implication is that Richard's Excalibur is either a deliberate fake, or that it was found in different and unknown circumstances. Without desiring to cast aspersions on England's glorious Lion-heart, the former seems more likely.

Certainly, later chroniclers were not always reluctant to contradict the story of Excalibur in Sicily. The English victory at Agincourt was of such national significance that a story soon arose which claimed that Henry V, known to be interested in the traditions of chivalry, had a mysterious 'Sword of Arthur' hidden in his baggage with other valued items. While never explicitly called Excalibur, the almost talismanic presence of an Arthurian sword at Agincourt both explains and provides an almost mystical nature to the famous victory, placing it within the context of England's legendary past and imperial destiny. Arthur's martial reputation could be invoked in less glorious situations than Agincourt, however, and even without claiming a particular object a family could partake in the glorious history of Camelot through other means.

ARTHURIAN HERALDRY

As we have seen, English monarchs were almost always eager to associate themselves with Arthur; the Angevin and Plantagenent kings in particular were interested in tracing (or creating) their descent from Britain's most famous king. The *Genealogies of Edward King of Britain* make Edward IV's descent from Arthur crystal clear and accord Edward a respect reserved elsewhere in the document only for Arthur, his Trojan ancestor Brutus and his ill-fated successor Cadwallader. The Mortimer family, powerful lords whose lands straddled the Welsh border and who periodically laid claim to the throne, based these claims in large part on their imagined descent from Arthur and Cadwallader; the fact that they also controlled Caerleon, the ancient Roman city associated with Arthur's coronation, added further lustre to their claims. Arthur's own arms, three golden crowns on *gules* (red) or *azure* (blue), appeared frequently in the propaganda of the medieval monarchy. Edward's own heraldic device was three suns on a red background and in one manuscript, the *Illustrated Life of Edward IV*, these suns are directly linked with Arthur's three crowns.

Heraldry in the Middle Ages was a serious business, governed by well-established rules, and in England was overseen by the Court of Chivalry, through which the royal constable and marshal of England examined chivalric issues both at home and on the continent. The court's most famous case was a dispute between Sir Richard Scrope and Sir Robert Grosvenor concerning the right to a particular heraldic device, the arms *azure* with *bend d'or*. The case is most famous today due to the involvement of one Geoffrey Chaucer, who was called as one of the witnesses by the presiding knight, Sir John de Derwentwater. John of Gaunt, the uncle of Richard II and father of Henry IV, also gave testimony to the court. Scrope and Grosvenor had only discovered that they shared the device while on campaign in 1385; the case dragged on for six years, with the Court finally deciding in favour of Scrope. Grosvenor was ordered to adopt new arms and further to pay damages.

The case was not an isolated one, with at least seven similar cases being tried in the fourteenth century alone.

Scrope himself had been involved in a previous trial involving the same heraldic device and although the records for this earlier incident are lost, John of Gaunt helpfully recalls the events for us. During Gaunt's campaign in France in 1373, Scrope had encountered a Cornish knight named Thomas Carminowe who also bore the arms *azure* with *bend d'or*. On this occasion, the Court of Chivalry found in favour of both litigants: apparently, because the families derived their arms from different nations, they could both keep them. Scrope's family had used this device since the Norman Conquest, while Carminowe had argued chronological precedence: his family had been granted their heraldic arms by King Arthur himself. Of particular importance for our purposes is that this Arthurian connection was not only accepted, it was also never seriously questioned. A direct familial inheritance from the distant Arthurian era was considered to be admissible and convincing evidence in the setting of the court.

The vogue for Arthurian heraldry began in the twelfth century and, with a brief lull in the late fourteenth, continued until the end of the Middle Ages. By 1300, there were at least 30 stable Arthurian heraldic devices, meaning that 30 of Arthur's knights were attributed with the same coat of arms in most Arthurian texts. Recent work by Michel Pastoreau confirms that, by the sixteenth century, there were 178 Arthurian heraldic devices and that attempts were being made by authors and illustrators to maintain a consistency across texts and in illuminations. Armorials were produced which helped to create this consistency and many of them survive. Arthur's arms of three golden crowns illustrates this consistency in a paradoxical manner: a misreading in an unidentified text results in all fifteenth-century French armorials assigning a device of 13 crowns to Arthur. Gawain and his brothers all bear a double-headed eagle on *purpure* (purple), with a variety of bars and stripes to differentiate between them (the correct heraldic term for this is, in fact, to 'difference' a device). Gawain's device in *Sir Gawain and the Green Knight*, the famous golden pentangle on *gules*, is not attested elsewhere and has more to do with the poem's central theme of inescapably connected virtues than any serious attempt at changing the character's traditionally assigned device. Heraldry acted to stabilise the chivalric community: individual knights could be identified through visual reference, either at tournament or on the battlefield. To some extent, Arthurian heraldry added a realistic touch to stories about the king even as they stabilised the 'history' of Arthur's reign; this history, after all, was also that of Europe and the west.

THE WEDALE RELICS

Connected with heraldic matters are the ostensibly more straightfor-ward, yet still mysterious, Wedale Relics. Associated with an unidentified place called Wedale, perhaps near Melrose in the Scottish borders, these relics were said to be the fragments of an image of the Virgin Mary, brought back from Jerusalem by Arthur. The story of Arthur's pilgrim-age to Jerusalem is told, in full, only in a manuscript of Nennius and even then it is a later addition to the text. In most versions of Arthur's conquering career he does not make it as far as Rome. Even the intrepid Leland never saw these fragments, but rather he learned of them from the unique addition to Nennius, possibly of the thirteenth century. The actual location of Wedale is itself unknown, although Glennie believed it was Stow, a few miles north-west of Melrose, which had a church dedicated to St Mary.

As Ditmas points out, there 'was a very early tradition that Arthur car-ried an image of the Virgin Mary into battle', as Geoffrey of Monmouth had made the claim that the image was on the inside of Arthur's shield (a motif also associated with Gawain in *Sir Gawain and the Green Knight*). Nennius had said that Arthur carried the image of the Virgin on his shoulders at a battle at a mysterious castle called Guinnion. Arthur continued to be associated with the heraldic device of the Virgin and Child and Ditmas believed that the 'story of the Wedale relics seems to be an attempt to rationalise the tradition' just at the moment when Arthur begins to assume a new coat of arms, the three or 13 azure crowns which represent his various conquests.

A politically and historically savvy argument might firmly link Arthur's azure crowns with English military ambitions and this in turn might prompt us to consider the location of the Wedale Relics. The Scottish borders were an area of frequent military activity. English and

Scottish alike glared at each other over its length and breadth, raided each other's homes and sacked each other's towns. One side or the other might well have thought to play up a story which linked Christendom's greatest saint, the mother of God and England's greatest king through a single object of veneration and protection: given the English appropriation of Arthur, it was likely to have been them.

If this symbolic alliance between England's ancient monarch and the Queen of Heaven herself could protect English borders, so too could Arthur's other heraldic device make claims on behalf of the English crown. King's Town (the modern Kingston-upon-Hull) was founded by Edward I on the banks of the Humber in 1299 and was given the same coat of arms as Arthur: three gold crowns on a blue field. The Humber was a significant river for medieval English historians: according to Geoffrey, only the Thames and the Severn could equal it in importance. Just as the Severn divided England from Wales, so the Humber was England's traditional northern boundary, as attested not only by Geoffrey and his followers but by the Anglo-Saxon historian Bede in his *Ecclesiastical History of the English People*.

In the French *Lancelot* prose romances, Lancelot conquers a hostile castle on an island in the Humber (no such island exists in reality) and Malory tells us that this castle, called Joyous Garde, is three days from Carlisle and possibly to be identified as either Alnwick or Bamborough. Lancelot's conversion of the castle on the Humber from a place of hostility towards to Arthur to a place of friendship heralds his arrival as a full member of Arthur's court, at least until he in turn will be besieged by the angry king after rescuing the queen from execution. The Humber always represents the northern limits of Arthur's effective power, as it often represented the effective limit of English power. That some on the border (Edward I and the monks of Wedale among them) might be interested in highlighting that power through Arthurian relics and heraldry should not surprise us. By now, we recognise the pattern.

ARTHUR AT UNIVERSITY

Aristocratic families were not the only corporate entities eager to wrap themselves up in Arthurian pageantry. Cambridge University also claimed a connection with Arthur, and although that connection might have begun as a joke, it is one that had serious consequences.

In the early fifteenth century, Nicholas Cantelupe wrote the *Historiola de antiquitate et origine almae et immaculatae Universitatis Cantebrigiae* (the *Little History of the Antiquity and Origin of the Nourishing and Immaculate University of Cambridge*). This text was the latest round in an ongoing battle between Cambridge and its great rival Oxford: each university wished to present itself as of greater antiquity (and thus greater respectability) than the other.

Oxford was, in reality, founded in the late twelfth century. It was certainly the oldest English university, but had been on the continent preceded by the medical academy at Salerno (the eleventh century) and the legal university at Bologna from early in the twelfth century. Geoffrey, however, had mentioned the town of Oxford as the home of one Sir Boso of Rydychen, which the Saxons would later name 'Oxenford'; Boso, the reader is told, is one of Arthur's many knights. Boso fights in many of Arthur's battles and even accompanies Gawain on an embassy to the Roman Emperor Lucius Hiberius. When the Emperor's nephew begins insulting the Britons, Gawain grows angry and kills him; Boso fights bravely alongside him. Geoffrey never emphasises Oxford for its learning. Rather, it is Boso whose actions take precedence. Subsequent writers, especially those associated with Oxford, were not so circumspect. Geoffrey had made no such claim for rival Cambridge and his testimony to Oxford's antiquity would later be picked up by the historians of the fourteenth century: Ranulph Higden would insist that Oxford had been founded by the English monarch, Alfred the Great, in 886. Alfred's posthumous reputation as a patron of learning led to the assumption by Oxford historians that he must have founded the ancient University of Oxford. Who else could have done so? Further claims in the French *Lancelot* cycle that Merlin's scribes included the future master of the first school at Oxford both confirmed and extended Oxford's enviable antiquity.

For Cambridge, famously founded by a group of Oxford dons who had murdered a prostitute and then fled the town, the need to create a more respectable and venerable origin proved irresistible. As Ad Putter remarks, a modern response to the Oxford origin story would have been to attempt to disprove it, but history, and history writing, did not work that way in the Middle Ages. Instead, historians sought to outdo their rivals, to trump their claims with ever more grandiose claims of their own (much as Scrope and Carminowe, and later Scrope and Grosvenor, would try and do). An early attempt at providing Cambridge with an ancient provenance appeared in a chronicle from Jervaulx Abbey, which noted the foundation of an East Anglian school during the reign of Sigeberht, mentioned by Bede in his influential *Eccesiastical History* (the chronicler also speculates that Bede himself founded Cambridge). Oxford fought back by claiming that Oxford's original name, Cricklade, really meant 'Load of Greeks', implying that the school (called Cricklade College and only later Oxford) had been founded by Greek scholars following the Trojan Brutus. Check and checkmate: after all, how could Cambridge hope to claim an antiquity predating Britain's mythological founder?

Nicholas Cantelupe, it seems, rose to the challenge with some aplomb. Noting the similarity between Cambridge ('Cantabrigia' in Latin) and the Spanish region of Cantabria, Cantelupe theorised that the founders of Cambridge were Spanish and he found an incident in Geoffrey which confirmed his theory: Geoffrey tells us that Ireland ('Hibernia') was founded by Partholaym, a warlord from Spain ('Hiberia'). Cantelupe gives Partholaym a brother, conveniently called Cantebrus, who accepts the invitation of the British king to join the latter's council, having decided not to travel all the way to Ireland. Cantelupe gives the fantastic date of 4321 years since Creation, which beat even Bede's date of AD 636. A school called Cambridge was better than an anonymous school; but in any event, Cantelupe argued, they were the same school after all. Better still, Cantelupe could now reverse history: Cambridge scholars, it could be argued, settled at Cricklade in order to help the struggling college. When Alfred founds Oxford, he can do so only because Cambridge laid the true foundations. Cantelupe provides a history of Cambridge in which many famous kings and popes contribute to the growing university and King Arthur is one of them.

Arthur appoints Kynot as proctor of Cambridge; the exact identity of Kynot is, as Putter notes, unknown, but might refer to a Kinocus found in Geoffrey as a priest who receives an undoubtedly welcome promotion. Geoffrey meant an archbishop's throne, but Cantelupe seems to have sent Kynot into an ivory tower instead. This Kynot is the recipient of a charter that outlines Cambridge's exemption from taxes and other royal burdens. Arthur honours Cambridge further by sending Gawain himself to bring the charter. This document miraculously survives Arthur's fall and the sacking of the university:

> But alas! After the death of the famous King Arthur, Cambridge, the city that was full of people, the mother of virtues, is widowed from her doctors because of the envy of warriors, the plundering of books, and the destruction of enemies. Thus the heinous Ambrones, the Picts and Saxons, invited by that traitor Mordred, destroy alike the Christian students and the citizens of Cambridge with sword and fire, as wolves destroy sheep.

Thus the age-old enmity between town and gown, so prominent in the actual history of medieval university life, is eclipsed by the jealous power of strong-armed warriors dedicated to the utter destruction of learning itself. No wonder, we might think, that North American universities are so keen to recruit athletes through scholarships rather than risk leaving them to their own devices. Cambridge, fortunately for Cantelupe, recovers from this disaster, and King Æthelbert of Kent, himself the descendant of the 'heinous … Saxons', but now a Christian, restores the university and confirms the privileges given to it by former monarchs, most prominently Arthur.

It does not concern us, in the present book, how Oxford rallied its own historiographical resources and managed to extend its own antiquity back to 1025 BC. Rather, we need to look closely at a remarkable document that was produced around 1510: a copy of the charter granted to Cambridge by Arthur and long-reputed as the university's oldest surviving document. Dyer printed a copy in 1824, among other documents relating to Cambridge; an illustrated copy dating from 1587 can still be seen today. This charter was used as a legal document, most famously against the Bishop of Ely when he tried to assert episcopal authority over Cambridge in the fifteenth century (it might be argued that the document was created for this occasion). Only in 1608, as antiquaries began to debate the relationship between Oxford and Cambridge with something resembling modern academic rigour, was Cantelupe's Arthurian claim disproved. Brian Twyne, an Oxford academic, finally confronted Cantelupe's evidence directly: he came to the conclusion that the Arthurian charter could not be authentic due to the fact that Arthur did not sign his name in the same fashion as he had done on the wax seal held at Westminster Abbey: and furthermore, the Cambridge Arthur only styles himself the king of England, ignoring Gaul, Germany and Dacia. It is a testament to the strength of the belief in the historicity of Arthur still held in the seventeenth century that the technical details of one forgery could be used in order to discredit another forgery.

TRISTRAM AND CURTANA

In 1207 a sword said to have been that of Tristram appeared in a list of King John's regalia; this item is never mentioned again, prompting some scholars to assume that it must have disappeared. Others have not been so certain, among them R.S. Loomis (who first discovered the passage in question) and Ditmas. They believed that this sword became Curtana or Curtein, one of the three swords later carried in coronation ceremonies of Eleanor of Provence, Henry III's queen, in 1236, although known there as the sword of St Edward the Confessor. Curtana, which has appeared in coronation ceremonies ever since (even if the sword must be remade from time to time), was known as the Sword of Mercy by 1483 (the others being the Sword of Justice Spiritual and the Sword of Justice Temporal). The right to carry Curtana could be jealously sought: Edmund of Lancaster, brother of Edward I, claimed the right to carry the sword at the latter's coronation and apparently decided not to appear at the ceremony after his claim was rejected. Piers Gaveston participated in the coronation of his friend Edward II, where a later Earl of Lancaster was permitted to carry Curtana; Gaveston, however, 'redeemed' the sword, a phrase which probably indicates his responsibility for returning Curtana to safe-keeping, which might be related to his role as chief chamberlain, an office he may have held at the time of the coronation.

Traditionally, Curtana was a shortened and blunted weapon, which was perhaps the primary reason for its attribution as the Sword of Mercy. Its early association with Tristram might also be based on this feature, for the sword Tristram used in his first battle (with the Irish champion Marhaus or the Morholt) was famously damaged during the fight:

Thus they fought stylle togydirs more than halffe a day, and eythir of them were wounded passynge sore, that the blood ran downe fresshly uppon the grounde. By than sir Trystramys wexed more fyerser than he [Marhaus] dud, and syr Marhalte fyebled, and sir Trystramys ever more well-wynded and bygger. And with a myghty stroke he smote sir Marhalte uppon the helme suche a buffete that hit went thorow his helme and thorow the coyffe of steele and thorow the brayne-panne [skull], and the swerde stake so faste in the helme and in his brayne-panne that sir Trystramys pulled three tymes at his swerde or ever he myght pulle hit oute from his hede.

And there sir Marhalte felle downe on his kneis, and the edge of his [Tristram's] swerde leffte in hys brayne-panne. And suddeynly sir Marhalte rose grovelyng and threw away his swerde and his shylde frome hym, and so ran to his shyppes and fledde his way.

Tristram recovers the arms of Marhaus and his own damaged sword, but the tip goes home with his Irish opponent.

Given this story, we can see how the sword of Tristram owned by King John might have possibly been seen to have symbolically represented England's domination of Ireland: John had famously invaded Ireland twice, first in 1185 and more successfully in 1210. Furthermore, John had been invested by his father Henry II as lord of English-controlled Ireland in 1177 at the Council of Oxford. While the extent of John's power and independence as lord of Ireland it is a matter of some debate, the association was nevertheless made. As Seàn Duffy notes, John was lord of Ireland for two and half times longer than he was king of England and eight times longer than he was Duke of Normandy. That he might have a sword associated with a famous victory over the Irish seems possible, if not probable, given the symbolic use of Arthurian objects that we have seen. The propaganda value would have been high in England, even if the interest of the native Irish in Arthurian stories was neither intense nor consistent.

Matthew Paris later calls the sword Curtein, which was also the name of the sword of Ogier the Dane. Ogier was one of Charlemagne's Twelve Peers and a companion of the more famous Roland, but he had also once been a knight of the Round Table. In one story he had been taken to Avalon by Morgan le Fay, where he slept until he was summoned forth to participate in Charlemagne's wars against the Saracens in Spain; in the thirteenth-century Prose *Tristan*, we find a story in which Ogier's sword Curtein is said to have once belonged to Tristram. Once again we see the medieval desire to provide an Arthurian provenance to a famous sword, highlighting the intense desire to make the Arthurian past real.

John's sword came from the German regalia that originally belonged to his grandmother, the Empress Matilda. The only explicit reference to the sword of Tristram is found in the 1207 Patent Rolls, when Peter des Roches, Bishop of Winchester and royal treasurer, acknowledges that he had received regalia items including a 'great crown which came from Germany'. Matilda had been the widow of the Holy Roman Emperor Henry V and the daughter of Henry I of England; she had contested the crown with Stephen of Blois and in the treaty which ended the civil war between them Stephen kept the crown on condition that Matilda's son Henry succeeded him. Her children by her second marriage, to the Count of Anjou, were the Angevin monarchs. Their interest in Arthurian material has already been discussed, but in particular the early Angevins were extremely interested in the Tristram story, linked as it was with the very beginning of the romance and chivalric genres.

John, campaigning against the East Anglian barons in 1216, stayed at Wishbech Castle while his baggage train made the long journey around the Wash. The traditional story is that a tide came in suddenly and everything, including the royal regalia, was lost; some stories even imply that John was present at the disaster. John died a few days later at Newark and no regalia associated with John has ever been found. The story, however, remains unproven and the links between Tristram's sword and Curtana must remain a matter for speculation. The current swords were made for the coronation of Charles II and were designed according to a medieval pattern to replace the regalia destroyed by Oliver Cromwell's agents following his rise to power. Like the destruction of Arthur's tomb at Glastonbury during the Reformation, the medieval Curtana was the victim of a regime bent on making a radical break with its past; objects which existed only to point to the past could not be allowed to survive.

A TWO-EDGED SWORD

The sword given to Tancred and the sword hidden in the baggage of Henry V at Agincourt are, like many of the relics we examine in this book, now lost to the mysteries of time. But even if they still existed, their antiquity would now have been re-dated and their provenance reconsidered. The College of Heraldry will not seriously entertain the Arthurian pretensions of any family, Carminowe or otherwise and indeed no family would make the claim in any event. Cambridge and Oxford, in their endless quest to outdo one another, eventually changed the parameters of the debate itself and in the process helped to destroy the naïve belief in Arthur's existence. Caxton's proofs were becoming liabilities.

The time of the Arthurian fraud, and the influence of these relics on English and continental politics, was fast coming to an end; the new learning associated with the court of the Tudors and their successors would explode pious Arthurian myths even as Henry VIII and Elizabeth I occasionally made excited reference to them in relation to their own power. Rusty swords and forged charters would no longer be enough to spark serious debate about Arthur or any other legendary aspect of British history. Indeed, the Arthurian relics we have examined (and new ones discovered down to the present day) would play a role in a far more limited debate: whether or not Arthur even existed. The days in which Arthur's existence could be taken for granted, and any ancient object therefore associated with him, were almost over. Yet even at this late stage, new Arthurian relics could still be created or rediscovered and the royal monastic house of Westminster Abbey would play a dominant role in the continuing legacy of Arthur.

5

Gilding the lily: Arthur and English royal authority

One might expect that, aside from Arthur's bones and perhaps his sword Excalibur, the most prized Arthurian relic would have been Arthur's crown or some other symbol of his regal authority. It might therefore be surprising that, while some claims were made concerning Arthur's crown and his signet ring, they apparently played a curiously small role in contemporary English politics. Were these items, both held at Westminster Abbey and both now lost, really of such little significance, or have we interpreted their importance in the wrong way? If the crown presented at Westminster really belonged (or at least was genuinely thought to have belonged) to Llywelyn and his predecessor Arthur, we might need to reconsider the story: the crown might have been more important to Edward than the Stone of Scone. Loomis thought it was 'obvious that Edward regarded the possession of Arthur's crown as symbolising his sovereignty over Wales, just as in 1296 he removed the coronation Stone of Scone to Westminster and in 1299 seized the crown of John Balliol to signify his overlordship of Scotland.' It is difficult to avoid the conclusion that the episode of Arthur's crown provided the model for Edward's later actions concerning the stone. For us the crown seems like a footnote, but to Edward and Langtoft it may well have been of great importance as an attempt at asserting symbolic control over the troublesome region of Wales.

CONTESTING ARTHUR'S CROWN

In 1284, Prince Alphonso, the ten-year-old heir to Edward I, solemnly presented a golden crown at the shrine of Edward the Confessor at Westminster. This act was meant to end decades of unrest in Wales, a situation that had revolved around the independent Welsh dynasty of Gwynedd in North Wales. The last ruler of this house, Llywelyn ap Gruffydd, had been killed in battle at Builth in 1282 by an English contingent led by Roger Lestrange and including a knight named Stephen Frankton; Frankton killed Llywelyn with his lance, apparently not recognising him and thus failing to take the prince prisoner. Edward would have paid good money for a live Llywelyn, if only for the pleasure of executing him afterwards. Llywelyn's brother and heir Dafydd had been captured within months and executed in Shrewsbury in 1283. Edward mercifully let the children of the dynasty live, the daughters in nunneries and the sons in prison; Dafydd's son Owain was kept in a wooden cage outside of Bristol Castle, from which he occasionally made requests to be allowed to play inside the castle walls.

Six months later, on 19 March 1284, Edward I issued the statute of Rhuddlan, which provided for the political settlement of the conquered territories; it was at Rhuddlan that Edward had received the head of Llywelyn, identified as such well after the battle. It is possible that Frankton himself, credited with personally striking the Welsh prince down, was the very man who subsequently identified and sent Llywelyn's head and possibly his crown. Another source indicates that the man who had beheaded Llywelyn was one Robert Body, but he may have decapitated the corpse after the Welsh prince's death. The crown was not the only piece of Welsh regalia to enter Edward's possession at this time: the Neith Cross, reputed to be a piece of the True Cross, was presented by a clerk formerly in the service of Llywelyn, Hugo ap Ythel, who used his reward money to finance his studies at Oxford. Edward is recorded as having had a dinner service made from other items found in Llywelyn's treasury and he adorned the Neith Cross considerably, using it in his private worship, as Edward IV was to also to do in the fifteenth century. Llywelyn's crown also underwent modifications after coming into Edward's hands. Within a month of the Rhuddlan statute, a record for the receipt and delivery of various items of plate and jewellery records the following:

> Item, for working up and gilding the crown of Llywelyn 6s. 8d., delivered to Matthew de Columbariis on Thursday after the feast of St Alphegus in April, 12 Edward I [20 April 1284].

Clearly, Edward knew that he had in his possession the crown of the last native Welsh prince and that to deposit this crown at Westminster was to effectively end all hopes for a Welsh political revival. The gilding of the crown seems to be important in the context of the presentation. It was not enough to ceremonially present the Welsh crown to St Edward's shrine: the crown had to appear to be worthy of the occasion.

However, either Edward himself or someone close to him did not consider this act, in itself, to be quite enough. Instead, the chroniclers attached to his reign provided a quite different provenance for this particular treasure. Pierre de Langtoft stated that the crown had been Arthur's and the English chronicler Robert Mannyng had later agreed with the statement in his translation of Langtoft. Certainly, the wardrobe record cited earlier claims only that the crown is Llywelyn's, not Arthur's; furthermore, the claim that Llywelyn's crown was Arthur's might be an ironic comment on the pretensions of an arrogant Welsh vassal. The Brabançon chronicler, Lodewijk von Veltham, who was attached to the English court, ended his inaccurate and romanticised story of Edward's conquest of the Welsh by relating a curious story: at the end of the campaign, Edward and his men descend into a cave where they see the bones of King Arthur. As we recall from chapter 3, only six years previously had Edward and his queen visited Glastonbury and participated in a ceremony in which Arthur's bones were exhumed, inspected and reburied in a magnificent sepulchre in the abbey itself. While von Veltham is alone in telling the story of Edward's seco... discovery of Arthur's bones, and perhaps has even failed to und... the original story, he still unwittingly testifies to the continu...

concerning Arthur, the Welsh and the English king. Apparently, one can never remind Edward's subjects often enough that he had seen the legendary king's skeleton: Arthur was not coming back and his legacy of imperial domination and associated symbols were now the property of the English monarchy. To understand what Edward hoped to gain from this, and how widely the story was believed, we need to examine the context in which the ceremony was held at Westminster on that distant April morning.

Llywelyn ap Gruffydd was one of the greatest leaders produced by the medieval Welsh. An astute politician who managed to effectively unite Wales under his personal rule, he used that position to play a dangerous political game with the English, occasionally submitting to the English monarch but sometimes acting in open defiance. Llywelyn had married Eleanor de Montfort, daughter of the notorious rebel baron Simon de Montfort, in 1278, after a long delay when she had been captured by a Cornish knight, Thomas Larchdeacon, in the Bristol Channel three years earlier. Llywelyn had been an ally of de Monfort during the latter's rebellion, known as the Barons' War, against Henry III, and Edward I was quite content to keep Eleanor de Montfort under his control following her capture. Llywelyn's title, Prince of Wales, had been acknowledged by Henry III in 1265 and that acknowledgement was reiterated by Edward I in 1277, even after Llywelyn had refused three times to do homage to the new king. His rule only ended when his brother Dafydd revolted in 1282, forcing Llywelyn to either join the rebellion or risk losing control of his own battle-eager followers.

Dafydd's sudden revolt was unexpected and treacherous. Coming to visit Roger Clifford at Harlech for Easter, he appeared at the castle on the eve of Palm Sunday and committed a massacre in the middle of the night. When he was sentenced to death in 1283, the court made much of Dafydd's timing: murder was one thing, murder during the holy feast of Easter quite another. Yet Dafydd's assault on Harlech was accompanied by other incidents: Oswestry, Aberystwyth, Carreg Cennen and Llandovery were all attacked in the space of a week. Llywelyn, who faced a difficult task balancing the English threat and the independence of his own vassals, could be ruthless: his older brother Owain had been imprisoned by him for over 20 years. The line of independent Welsh princes ended with Llywelyn. While the Welsh poet Gruffudd ab yr Ynad Coch noted that many cried on Llywelyn's last battlefield just as their forebears had wept at Camlann, Arthur's last battlefield, the presence of Welsh troops in Edward's forces and a list of Welsh complaints given to Edward after 1282 hinted that the Welsh were not universally enamoured of the last native prince.

Wales was very different from Edward's England, a fact that Edward and his followers consistently failed to recognise. The Marches, with their strong regional lords ostensibly loyal to the English crown, resembled the feudal model prevalent in England and on the continent. North Wales, where Gwynedd was located, was dominated by the Black Mountains and the rugged coast; villages and manors were remote and tended to self-sufficiency over trade and what trade there was often based on barter rather than money. Edward's laws, imposed on the Welsh after 1282, often failed to take the geography and economy of the region into account: the law demanding that one person from each household come to a local market once a week was bound to cause hardship for isolated communities. Demands for surplus grain were difficult for a pastoral economy to provide and Llywelyn's castle-building program in the 1270s had already strained native resources. Edward spent far more time and money building the ring of magnificent castles around the region than Llywelyn ever could; one of Edward's castles, Caernarfon, was the location of the birth of his fourth son, the future Edward II. That Edward I could claim that this fulfilled a promise to the Welsh concerning a return to rule by a native-born infant prince testifies to his dismissive and arrogant policy in the conquered territory.

PRINCE(S) OF WALES

Within a year of the crown's presentation at Westminster, Alphonso would be dead. His infant brother Edward of Caernarfon, the only son of Edward I and his first wife Eleanor of Castile to live to adulthood, became the heir to the throne of England. In 1301, Edward I would confer the title of Prince of Wales upon this second Edward, a practice which was henceforth associated with the heirs to the British throne (sporadically at first but with increasing regularity down to the present day). But it might be that Edward had conceived a similar plan for Alphonso in the immediate aftermath of the 1282 conquest, hinting that the strategy was a well-considered one and connected with the same kind of Arthurian propaganda Edward brought to bear when he re-interred Arthur and Guinevere at Glastonbury. Edward and his surviving son were often at odds: Edward's exile of his son's friend and possible lover Piers Gaveston was only the beginning of a strain in their relationship. Further, while Edward of Caernarfon was an excellent horseman, he preferred rural pursuits to martial ones: he was known to enjoy digging ditches, building hedges and other work associated with peasants. While this man-of-the-people image might be fine in a modern American president, it plays less well in a medieval English court. Rumours of homosexuality with Gaveston and a very public dispute with Walter Langton, Bishop of Coventry and royal treasurer, whose property the younger Edward broke into in 1305, caused a rift between father and son. All of this lay in the future: in the meantime, a standard English royal practice connected with Edward's successful extinction of the native Welsh princes had been created and Edward II, despite never visiting Wales after his investiture as prince, was able to rely on substantial Welsh support during the troubles which ended his own reign.

In the late fourteenth-century poem *The Awntyrs of Arthure* (or *The Adventures of Arthur at Tarn Wadling*), the traditionally childless Arthur comes closest to actually naming an heir. A brief summary is required for those who have not read this poem. Arthur and his court, including Gawain and Guinevere, decide to go hunting near Carlisle, near the Scottish border. Gawain and Guinevere become separated from the rest of the court by a storm and they are confronted by a ghost in the midst of a burning lake; the ghost is Guinevere's mother, allowed a brief respite from the tortures of the damned in order to warn her daughter about the perils of pride. At the same time, she warns Gawain that his uncle Arthur's aggressive military policies will eventually result in the destruction of the Round Table. Subsequently reunited, the court returns to Carlisle for dinner. Festivities are interrupted by the appearance of a beautiful woman and a knight; the knight's name is Galeron and he now claims that his lands (Galloway) has been unjustly taken by Arthur and given to Gawain. The two knights fight a long battle, with Gawain the eventual winner. Guinevere, alert to the anguish of Galeron's lady and of the suffering of the two knights, pleads with Arthur to make a truce between the two knights. In return for his nephew Gawain's restoration of Galloway to its original lord Galeron, Arthur gives Gawain, among other lands, 'the worship of Wales at wil and at wolde'.

Galeron's battle with Gawain only occupies the second half of *Awntyrs*, the first half concentrating on the appearance of the ghost of Guinevere's mother before Gawain and the queen. Her warning to her daughter revolves around pride in one's appearance and love of splendour, both of which lead to suffering in the afterlife. The ghost's warning to Gawain is concerned with Arthur's covetous nature and his military pride, predicting the war with the Romans and Mordred's usurpation. Twice she counsels Gawain to take heed of her warnings, telling him openly that Arthur's incessant lust for military conquest will be the ruin of the Round Table and the death of Gawain himself. She even mentions that:

> In rich Arthur's hall,
> The bairn [child] plays with a ball
> That shall undo you all,
> Sadly on that day.

This child, unnamed, is Mordred: the ghost's prophecies are hauntingly specific, but no warning is given without at least the chance to avoid them. Following their return to court, Guinevere arranges for masses to be sung for her mother's ghost and Gawain is caught up in his battle with Galeron.

The twin plots are concluded nicely by Guinevere's religious and filial devotion and by the new feudal arrangements ordered by Arthur. Arthur's gift of Wales is far more than compensation for the lands Gawain was given and which are now being returned to Galeron. Just as the masses are meant to redeem and restore the soul of Guinevere's mother, and eventually translate her from suffering to paradise, so too is Arthur's gift of Wales meant to stabilise the political situation. It is clear that Arthur is aware of the ghost's prophecies, since Guinevere 'tells them the wonders that they had seen there'. There are thus two intertwining interpretations of Arthur's gift and reconciliation and res- toration are the major themes of the *Awntyrs*. First, Gawain as Prince of Wales is being placated for the loss of the lands Arthur had given him earlier and now must take away for diplomatic reasons. Second, Arthur is tacitly acknowledging that Gawain is, to borrow a phrase, the rock upon which his kingdom's stability depends. By the time the *Awntyrs* is written, the title of 'Prince of Wales' for the heir to the English throne is standard: Edward III's son, the Black Prince, ensured that the title carried a prestige in later centuries. Gawain is Arthur's heir, just as Edward of Caernarfon was Edward I's heir, and as Alphonso had once been when he presented Llywelyn's, or Arthur's, crown at Westminster. The medieval reader could hardly fail to notice the echo of contemporary royal practice concerning the succession.

Arthur's actions provide a suitable response to the dire warnings of the ghost. First, his desire to conquer new lands is alleviated by his present willingness to restore Galeron's lands; even though he immediately wins back the knight's allegiance, Arthur has been magnanimous rather than covetous in his motivations. Second, even as Guinevere's masses imply the possibility of redemption after death and the notion that it is never too late to amend one's ways, so too the ghost's warnings to Gawain imply that he can, if he is on his guard, avoid the prophesied fate and stabilise the realm either by ameliorating the worst of Arthur's excesses or by surviving the fall of the Round Table and becoming king. Arthur's nomination of Gawain to the 'worship of Wales' is an astute attempt at establishing a political continuity and helps to provide a satisfactory ending to the poem, even if the knowledgeable reader knows that the prophecies of the ghost are fated to eventually come true despite Arthur's efforts to the contrary. His authority is, for the moment, unchallenged; his far-flung conquests are secure. Surely the English kings who thought their own authority descended from Arthur's would seek more physical proof of these territorial achievements, even as they, in practice, continued to ignore the ghost's warnings.

CRAZED IN PEECES: ARTHUR'S SEAL AT WESTMINSTER

In 1608 Brian Twyne, an Oxford historian trying to discredit a charter held at Cambridge in which King Arthur granted the later university a series of rights and privileges, turned to another Arthurian relic for support. In the Cambridge charter Arthur calls himself the king of England; but on a seal held at Westminster he describes himself as 'Patritius Arthurius, Britanniae, Galliae, Germaniae, Daciae Imperator, &c'. Why would Arthur, Emperor of Britain, Gaul, Germany and even distant Dacia refer to himself as a mere king of England on the Cambridge charter? Clearly, the charter must be a forgery. One Arthurian object is used to discredit another, hinting at a kind of hierarchy which can only dimly be understood; even in the seventeenth century the seal can be taken seriously, at least as long as it supports one's own argument.

The seal itself was an impressive artefact: Leland, who examined it in 1540, records that it showed appropriate signs of great age. It was made of red wax, into which, it was imagined, Arthur had pressed a signet ring or stamp. A crowned and robed Arthur was seated upon a half circle, 'such one as we see the raine boe is' says Leland. His right hand holds a sceptre capped with a fleur-de-lis and in the left is a traditional symbol of emperors associated with emperors since Rome's fall: a globe surmounted by a cross. His full beard testifies to his success in eluding beard-collecting enemies like King Ryons, the former owner of the sword Marmiadoise, and less facetiously hints at wisdom and strength. Medieval signet rings survive in great numbers: not only did every king have his own personal seal, so did bishops and other aristocrats. Seals were a means of assuring the continued privacy of communications, as a broken seal meant the document had been tampered with; drama and story contain incidents of seals broken and cunningly repaired, just as Hamlet intercepts the message containing orders for his own death in Shakespeare's play. But such interference seems to have been rare enough that seals continued to be used, and as implied in the description of Arthur's seal, the message contained in the image was just as important as the privacy it sometimes guaranteed. At least one observer claimed that the Westminster seal adorned a charter granted to the abbey itself, reminding us that a seal also acted as a signature in a time when handwriting was neither unique to the individual nor a guarantor of identity. The seal was Arthur's authority, imprinted for all to see and understand.

The wax itself was cracked, and in Leland's phrase 'crazed here and there into peeces', but the imprint was protected by a silver and crystal frame which revealed Arthur's title and showed a suitably majestic image of the ancient king. It seems as though the precious frame actually kept the seal together in addition to protecting it from the elements. It hung in the shrine of St Edward the Confessor, exactly where little Alphonso had once deposited Arthur's crown, and Christopher Dean believes this situation made the seal 'some kind of pseudo-religious relic'. As we have endeavoured to demonstrate, all relics are both religious and political; Arthur's regalia is simply farther towards the political side of the spectrum than a splinter of the True Cross such as the one contained within the Neith Cross.

The origins of Arthur's seal were a mystery even to these early observers. John Rastell, who saw the seal but doubted its authenticity, was told that the seal came from a charter granted to Westminster Abbey itself, but a mere decade later the guardians could not or would not say anything on the subject to the more sympathetic Leland. He concluded, reasonably enough, that the seal must have originally come from Glastonbury, a place Leland knew had been associated closely with Arthur's reign. Ditmas believed that the seal appeared 'during the hey-day of the Tudor cult of the Arthurian legend' but this cannot be true: Caxton, as we saw, testifies to its presence in 1485, the very year Henry Tudor came to the throne following his victory at Bosworth Field. This victory was by no means certain and, as we saw earlier, Henry Tudor's occupation of the throne was not entirely secure for some time after Bosworth. The hey-day of the Tudor cult of Arthur was to come well after 1485. The seal disappears during the Reformation when Westminster Abbey is dissolved and many other relics go missing. It is difficult to imagine such an item being destroyed by Arthur-conscious Tudors, but if doubt about the item had become widespread perhaps it was deemed best to let it slip away quietly. Of all of our Arthurian relics, the seal is perhaps most likely now to turn up in an attic somewhere.

THE FATE OF ARTHUR'S CROWN

The crown seems to vanish under different, earlier circumstances. One might expect Arthur's crown to have disappeared at the same time as the seal, but in the list of the abbey's relics compiled in 1467 it is not mentioned, nor is it mentioned in 1479 or 1520. Caxton does not mention it in his preface. There are two possible suspects in the disappearance of the crown, whether it was Arthur's or Llywelyn's: the perpetrators of the infamous 1303 burglary of Westminster, or Piers Gaveston, the favourite courtier of Edward II.

The story of 1303 theft is a fascinating one in itself. The crime seems to have been perpetrated by one Richard de Podlicote, with a little help from the inside: the Abbot of Westminster and 48 of his monks were indicted in the crime, although never punished for their alleged role. Podlicote, a merchant specialising in wool, butter and cheese, apparently took 98 days to dig a tunnel under the abbey grounds and once inside he forced his way into the treasury itself. His motivation was simple: he had been arrested in Flanders and forced to pay 14 pounds towards King Edward's debts in Bruges on the principle that any Englishman could be expected to assist his monarch with his financial difficulties (especially if that Englishman wanted to return home again). Podlicote, upon his return to England, had been just as unsuccessful as the merchants of Bruges in getting the sum back from the English king. The monks assisted in carrying the objects away out of simple greed, one imagines, although they left the crown jewels behind. Edward's great crown and coronation ring, as well as a seal associated with his father Henry, were left behind for reasons unknown. Perhaps they were thought to be too high profile to be pawned, which was the fate of most of the stolen treasure.

The robbery was only discovered when various goldsmiths began displaying the purchased items in their shops, and such notables as William Torel, designer of the funeral monuments of Henry III and Eleanor of Castile, were offered some of the pieces. Podlicote took most of the blame, having been found with £2,000 worth of stolen goods. He was hanged before being flayed alive, producing the story that his skin was then used to cover the treasury door; the latter part of this tale, at least, is very likely a grotesque legend influenced by the stories of the skins of Danes having been used to upholster the doors of churches. Most of the precious objects stolen seem to have been recovered shortly afterwards in London, Northampton and Chichester where they had been sold. In any event the legal records indicate that crowns were left alone – at least three others besides Edward's great crown went untouched – leaving Gaveston as the most prominent possibility.

Piers Gaveston had formed a close bond with Edward of Caernarfon, sometime after he was transferred to the young prince's household in 1300. They apparently fought together in the Scottish campaign that year, where it was reputed that they had sworn some kind of brotherly oath. The exact nature of their relationship is unknown and many have seen in their closeness the signs of a homosexual relationship. One chronicle archly reports that Edward's manner of execution, after his neglected wife and her lover Roger Mortimer had taken power, was a red-hot poker administered to a bodily area of both physical and symbolic sensitivity. Pierre Chaplais disagrees, arguing that there is no sign of either man being homosexual rather than simple blood-brothers; they both had children and Edward's father-in-law Philip the Fair would have been unlikely to give his daughter 'to a man whose ethics in love did not conform to the high standard which he expected of a son-in-law'. This proof seems hardly convincing and the further assertion that the Edward-Gaveston relationship was closer to that between Jonathan and David, or Achilles and Patroclus, seems inadequate given the later reputations of these other famous male friends. Gaveston's first exile from England in 1307 was, by most accounts, prompted by Edward I's anxiety over the closeness between the younger men: the *Chronicle* of John de Trokelowe will only say that 'certain reasons' were involved, but the *Annals of St Paul's* is more blunt, stating that Edward I knew that his son's excessive affection for Gaveston would be a source of trouble for the kingdom. Edward is said to have asked on his deathbed in the very year Gaveston had been exiled, that his counsellors ensure that Gaveston be prevented from returning. Once Edward was dead, Gaveston's return was among his son's very first acts as king. The year 1307, in the end, turned out to be a very good one for the up-and-coming Gascon knight.

The homosexuality or lack thereof is not very important to the argument outlined here, except that it is part and parcel of the real problem with Gaveston: Edward II gave him everything he could want. Gaveston was named Earl of Cornwall in Edward's first royal charter, apparently before he had even returned to England. The new earl, only recently exiled by the elder Edward, was literally welcomed into the family by the younger: Gaveston married his friend's niece Margaret de Clare, a wealthy heiress, in the year of his return. Gaveston was even made regent during the Edward's brief absence in January 1308, while the king was away getting married to a French princess named Isabella, even though the king had royal brothers by his father's second marriage, Thomas and Edmund, who were more than capable of holding the position. Gaveston was given wider powers than most regents had traditionally received, including the power to assent in ecclesiastical elections; under previous regents, the wealthier and larger churches had to wait until the monarch returned before their elections could be confirmed and oaths of fealty given. Gaveston was called 'England's second king' and as such, people believed he had helped himself to England's royal wealth.

The Ordinances of 1311 claimed that the royal treasure had almost entirely disappeared by the time Edward II was crowned in 1307; the author of the *Chronicle of the Civil Wars of Edward II* believed that, ultimately, the new king was himself responsible for the losses. The resulting lack of resources forced Edward II into an unpopular and unsustainable programme of excessive taxation, although it is possible to dismiss this as typical of chroniclers unwilling to directly criticise a reigning monarch. It is always safer to blame a courtier, especially one as powerful and widely hated as Gaveston. Walter of Guisborough first pinpointed the whereabouts of the stolen loot: Gaveston's native land, Gascony. John de Trokelowe believed that Gaveston's appropriations had begun during the reign of Edward I, when the Prince of Wales would give him presents from the treasury. Gaveston would send these valuables out of the country using foreign merchants as agents. Just after Gaveston's final arrest and execution on 4 May 1312, the Earl of Lancaster entered his last known whereabouts (Newcastle-upon-Tyne) and discovered a vast quantity of treasure. He later claimed that this was the missing royal treasure, contradicting his earlier insistence in the Ordinances that the treasure had gone overseas. That this hoard was largely, although not exclusively, royal treasure is certain; the king himself had been in Newcastle with Gaveston and had left it behind in a bid to save Gaveston from capture. As J.S. Hamilton wryly notes, Edward left his pregnant queen Isabella behind at the same time.

Chaplais believes that Gaveston is innocent of most of the charges against him, not just those of homosexuality. He has argued that those who accused Gaveston of theft 'misinterpreted some piece of evidence which established a link between Gaveston and the royal treasure'. He argues that Gaveston held the office of chief chamberlain and in that capacity would have acted as intermediary between the king and various petitioners. Therefore, far from usurping the king's authority, he was in fact representing it. Furthermore, he did not steal anything from the treasury, but was 'given' the treasure in his capacity as chamberlain. Chaplais argues that 'instead of being another illustration of Edward's alleged habit of lavishing valuable presents on Gaveston, it was simply designed to ensure the safe keeping of the gifts by sending them without delay to the royal chamberlain, who also happened to be at the time keeper of the realm'. An explanation that seems altogether very tidy and other scholars have tended to agree that the treasure found in Newcastle is a combination of Edward's personal treasures and Gaveston's own wealth.

There is undoubtedly an element of truth in Chaplais' argument. Clearly, Gaveston neither stole the entire contents of the royal treasury, nor did he send it all to Gascony. However, it may be that the mystery of the disappearance of Arthur's crown is entwined within this controversy. Within a few years of Edward I's death, some chroniclers are beginning to show scepticism about the connection between Arthur and Llywelyn's crown. Rishanger states that the king received the crown 'cum aliis jocalibus' ('with other jesting articles') and although the precise meaning of 'jocalibus' in this context is uncertain, Christopher Dean notes that that some later chroniclers did not take Langtoft's claims seriously. Certainly, the wardrobe record of the regilding of the crown asserts only that the crown is Llywelyn's, not Arthur's, and the claim that Llywelyn's crown was Arthur's might perhaps be read as an ironic comment on the pretensions of an arrogant Welsh vassal. Furthermore, while Gaveston might have been innocent of the charges of theft levelled against him, it is possible that he did indeed receive some of the royal treasure as gifts from Edward II: exactly those items which were seen by some as jokes in the first place. Rishanger is certainly wrong in writing the crown off as a frivolous joke: the crown was, at the very least, thought to be that of Llywelyn, and as such it would already have had great importance as a powerful piece of propaganda. Yet Rishanger reduces the entire matter to a jest.

We know that Edward II did not share his father's enthusiasm for Arthur, although his son and heir would. There is likewise no evidence that Gaveston showed any interest in Cornwall's Arthurian heritage, as an earlier earl (Edward I's uncle Richard of Cornwall, discussed in the next chapter) had done in an age when Tintagel Castle could be rebuilt for propaganda rather than defence. For Gaveston, Cornwall was important for the prestige of its title and the wealth of its tin mines, although it must be said that Gaveston enjoyed the chivalry of the tournament even if he showed little interest in the chivalry found in Arthurian romance. Given that we know that Edward II shared little of his father's enthusiasm for the Arthurian past, it is tempting to imagine that he and Gaveston might have seen the crown in a similar light, as a ridiculous artefact, and we can perhaps understand why Edward might have give his confidante and adopted brother a highly amusing trinket, that was said to have been Arthur's. After all, before he had been king, Edward of Caernarfon had been Prince of Wales. As such, surely the crown of the last independent Welsh prince, regardless of any mythic connotations, was his as well? If Gaveston was innocent of the charges of theft levelled against him, it is just possible that he did receive some of the royal treasure from Edward II, including exactly those items which were seen by some as jokes. Arthur's crown, increasingly ignored by commentators and probably taken seriously by very few, was Edward's to dispose of as he pleased. For his blood brother and possible lover, a man who enjoyed the thrill of the chivalric joust and was Earl of Cornwall, what could be a better gift than 'Arthur's gilded crown'?

A HIERARCHY OF KINGS: ARTHUR AND ST EDWARD THE CONFESSOR

The Great Seal at Westminster was certainly noticed by observers during its apparently brief existence and its inclusion in the shrine of St Edward the Confessor is suggestive. Edward, the last true Anglo-Saxon king, despite being half-Norman through his mother Emma, had been a surprisingly ineffective monarch, allowing Norman encroachments, the advancement of a powerful and nearly uncontrollable faction called the Godwins represented most famously at Hastings by Harold of Wessex, and failing even to father a son. It was sometimes exactly these ineffective kings which had the best cases for canonisation: even the vilified

Edward II and his father's great enemy Simon de Montfort attracted the attention of would-be worshippers from both friends eager to glorify their memory and enemies equally eager to minimise their role in the putative saint's downfall.

In Malory's time, Henry VI, son of the warrior-king Henry V, who once fell into a coma for two years upon learning that he had somehow impregnated his wife, became a candidate for sainthood in the years after his death in prison. Unlike other many other political saints, Henry's cult seems to have been widespread, moving out from the saint's focal shrine at St George's Chapel in Windsor Palace with astonishing speed: within a few decades, there were devotional shrines to Henry VI in Whimple, Devon; Ashton-under-Lyne near Manchester; Alnwick in Northumberland (a fortress which Malory associates with Lancelot's burial in the *Morte Darthur*); and throughout East Anglia. He was rapidly becoming the saint of failure and adversity: he was once credited with saving the life of Henry Walter de Guildford, a badly injured sailor who had been put out to sea by his shipmates after being shot with a cannonball. Henry VI was well on his way to rivalling Thomas Becket when his early Tudor support was abruptly ended by Henry VIII's Reformation.

Edward the Confessor, like Henry VI, was associated with a piety that both became him as a Christian but did not entirely suit him as a monarch. The extinction of his line through his childlessness, much like Arthur's traditional lack of legitimate heirs, enabled the Confessor to become the saint of the English monarchy: one of the dubious miracles associated with him was an angelic visitation confirming the future of the English kingdom if he chose William of Normandy as his successor. Surely it would be too cynical to note that the story only circulated after William came to the throne. Yet Edward's role deepened over time and almost every English monarch paid lip service to the cult of this most pious of forebears. Henry III was a particularly keen devotee, naming his son after the saint; a subsequent run of Edwards, ending with the uncrowned Black Prince, ensured that the Confessor would continue to play a role as patron of the royal bloodline and of the kingdom.

To deposit objects of another principality or kingdom in the shrine of St Edward was a supremely political act. When the Stone of Scone was presented to Westminster Abbey in 1296, it was accompanied south by other important symbols of Scottish independence; the Scottish king John Balliol's crown was just one piece of the Scottish regalia confiscated at that time. The enthronement Stone from Scone was placed beside the crown of Arthur, won for Edward I at the battle of Builth in 1282, and although the Stone of Scone would be returned some 700 years later, Arthur's crown would disappear forever. They were being given to the English king's sainted namesake and forebear, Edward the Confessor, as symbols of English lordship over the entire island of Britain. In a sense, the British Arthur was being subordinated to the English Confessor; after all, the older Edward was a real saint, with real relics. It was Arthur's death, not any potentially active afterlife in Heaven, which was emphasised in 1278 at Glastonbury and in 1282 at Westminster. Despite the later Edward's interest in Arthur and his secular relics, there was no eagerness to see the British king take a place among the saints, from which he might be just as likely to listen to Welsh prayers as English ones.

6

Counter-relics: objects from the Celtic edge

Thus far, this book has examined relics associated with Arthur found at English sites or held in English hands: the burial and reburials at Glastonbury, the Round Table at Winchester, the claims to Excalibur held by Richard Lionheart and Henry V. However, we must remember that Arthur is in origin a Celtic hero, a war-leader who traditionally held back the Anglo-Saxon ancestors of the English on behalf of the native British peoples. These early, shadowy wars ended with the Celts pressed back into Cornwall, Galloway, Brittany and Wales. How did these peoples subsequently remember Arthur?

For England's Welsh and Cornish neighbours, the historicity of Arthur, and to a similar extent Merlin, is inscribed on very fabric of the landscape itself. Welsh and Cornish sites associated with Arthur can often claim an older provenance than those in England and certain sites like Carleon and Carlisle are transferred into the English Arthurian tradition with little overt commentary by English scribes or historians. Malory might claim that Camelot became Winchester, but most Arthurian texts, even those written in English, do not make the same claim: Caerleon, although it was an unimportant provincial backwater as far as the English were concerned, was considered to be Arthur's capital by most interested English readers in the Middle Ages.

On those rare occasions when a physical relic associated with a Celtic location is mentioned in a medieval or early modern source, they are typically of a different nature than their English counterparts. We have seen that Llywelyn made no claims himself that his crown had ever been Arthur's, despite what Edward I and the English chroniclers later claimed, and while Llywelyn and his fellow Welsh princes may have indeed asserted a line of descent from Arthur, the legendary king's crown (like his body), remained lost to time. It was of course essential to the Celtic legends that Arthur's grave should remain undiscovered if he was to remain the source of future national hope. If Arthur was indeed dead and buried, he definitely could not return – a fact that was not lost on both Henry II and Edward I. At the same time, many of Arthur's most important knights – Gawain, Lancelot, Galahad – were either non-existent in the Welsh tradition, or essentially different characters altogether. When a Welsh or Cornish site lays claim to an association with one of Arthur's contemporaries, the person claimed is either linked with the area in the stories, in the manner of Queen Isolde of Cornwall, or nearly unknown in England, as we find with the various Celtic saints whose written *Lives* involved Arthur as ally, foe or relative.

THE CELTIC SAINTS

Wales, Cornwall and Brittany share a unique set of saints, local represent-atives of the heavenly community who, aside from the rare exception, did not become universally known or venerated. The place-names of these regions reflect the many obscure native-born saints who laboured to convert, console and educate the Celts in the centuries between the fall of Rome and the coming of the Normans. Today only a few of these saints are widely known and then only because the anonymous authors of their eleventh- and twelfth-century *Vitae* (*Lives*) chose to link them with the famous King Arthur. It must be observed, with some degree of irony, that many of these *Lives* do not represent a good relationship between Arthur and the saints who encounter him. Nevertheless, their fame, like that of many of the knights and heroes whose stories were absorbed into the growing Arthurian legend, lives on through their association with Arthur. Even when medieval writers criticise Arthur, they are well aware that his presence in their stories can raise public interest in their saint who must compete in the highly competitive world of hagiography. Just as Arthur's motivation for the uncovering of Brân's buried head was his pride, so his relationship with many Celtic saints was troubled by his arrogance.

The *Life of Cadog* records a story in which a man takes refuge with the saint after killing three of Arthur's men; while Arthur seems justified to our minds in pursuing the killer, medieval respect for the laws of sanctuary ensured that Cadog is quite right to humiliate the king. When Cadog summons three judges (St Teilo, St David and St Illtud) to judge the case, they decide that Arthur should be given some cattle in compensation, three or a hundred depending on the source. Not satisfied, Arthur insists that the cows be parti-coloured, red in front and white behind. Annoyed, Cadog miraculously changes a variety of cattle into the requested colours, but when the cattle reach Arthur and his men they turn into bundles of ferns. Another story tells of St Padarn's pilgrimage to Jerusalem, where the Patriarch of the holy city gives him a beautiful woven tunic. Upon his return home to live in a cell, Padarn meets Arthur, who demands the tunic for himself. Refusing to take no for an answer, Arthur is punished by being swallowed by the earth – up to his neck. He begs forgiveness and peace is restored. One might wonder about any links between Padarn's tunic and the Wedale Relics, discussed in chapter 4. These stories are simple and localised; Arthur's name adds a level of interest for the reader, but is largely not essential. Any nasty-tempered secular ruler would do. One story, however, has wider ramifications for the medieval legend and modern attempts to find the real Arthur.

St Gildas the wise is strongly associated with Arthurian history: he is known today for his *De Excidio et Conquestu Britanniae*, in which he laments the failure of the British people to hold back the Saxon invaders. He blames the kings of Britain and the sins of the people, but notoriously never mentions King Arthur even though Gildas himself tells us that he was born in the year of the Battle of Badon, traditionally Arthur's greatest victory. Scholars have taken Gildas as proof that Arthur did not exist, but that theory is complicated by the ninth-century Breton *Life of Gildas*, in which the monk mediates between Arthur and Melwas, kidnapper of Guinevere, as we discussed in chapter 2. Gildas intervenes despite his dislike of Arthur, who had killed the saint's brother, a pirate and rebel lord named Caw, a fact sometimes taken to explain Arthur's absence in the *Excidio*: Gildas hated Arthur so much that he excised him from history. All that can be said for certain is that Gildas was a real man living in the late sixth century and a rare witness to the events that ended the Celtic domination of the British Isles. His link to Arthur, unlike his link to Glastonbury, remains speculation; Gildas was not alone in attracting Arthurian elements into his own story, but the level of antagonism hinted at between Arthur and Gildas seems less superficial than the conflicts between Arthur and various British saints. The same might be said of saints friendlier to Arthur.

Gildas was a student of the less well-known St Illtud (*c.*450-535). A cousin of Arthur, Illtud was living with his father in Brittany when he decided to visit the court in about 470. It is an identifiable feature of the Arthurian tradition that Arthur gains cousins and nephews at a phenomenal rate as the legends develop. While at Arthur's court, Illtud marries a woman of the court, Trynihid, and serves in the war-band of a Welsh chieftain, Poulentus. After some years Illtud becomes disillusioned with the martial life and when a friend is killed while out hunting, he and his wife leave the court and became recluses. Illtud's strong reaction is explained in the *Life of St Cadoc*, where the hunting party rudely demands food of the saint; when they are later lost in a swamp and perish, their arrogance is given the blame. Illtud, separated from the main hunting party, is the sole survivor, and Illtud eventually becomes the disciple of either Dubricius, the legendary saint who conducted the ceremonies at the wedding of Arthur and Guinevere, or the historically attested Germanus of Auxerre (depending upon which story one reads), and is later renowned for his learning and wisdom. Many of the most prominent British saints, including Samson and Gildas, learn from Illtud. The *Life of Illtud*, written in about 1140, has a reputation for the marvellous matched rarely even by the typically miraculous genre of hagiography and in Wales his legend subsequently becomes even more amazing. Illtud's reputation develops until he is imagined to have been one of the guardians of the Holy Grail in the Welsh Triads and is even conflated with the 'best knight in the world', Galahad.

Warrior saints were far from unknown in the Middle Ages and the cults of such martial figures as George, Martin of Tours and the

Archangel Michael were extremely popular with knights. St George began life as a warrior-saint associated with dragon-slaying whose medieval legend records his martyrdom during Diocletian's persecution of the Christians, but who would later became the patron saint of England. When Edward III founded the Order of the Garter in 1348, he had a chapel dedicated to St George at Windsor and one might understand this moment as a key point in the process of George becoming the patron saint of England. We might also remember that Arthur himself fought a giant on Mont St Michel in Brittany during his campaign against the Romans (related in Malory and his sources), once again invoking the greatest of holy knights, St Michael. These stories point towards an engagement between the Arthurian legend and the cults of various warrior-saints that is also evidenced by the story of St Illtud and his even more obscure compatriots Pedrog and Derfel.

CAMLANN'S SAINTLY SURVIVORS: DERFEL THE MIGHTY AND PEDROG SPLINTER-SPEAR

In 1538, a Franciscan friar named John Forest was burned to death for heresy at Smithfield. Forest had been the confessor of Queen Catherine of Aragon, the first wife of Henry VIII and had been kept under arrest since 1534. Forest had, at the age of 20, received the habit of St Francis at Greenwich and joined a strict branch of the Franciscans known as the Observants. After studying at Oxford, he later became one of the chaplains of Queen Catherine of Aragon, the first wife of Henry VIII, and was eventually appointed her confessor.

Forest's career was a stormy one even before his martyrdom, as in 1525 he was threatened with excommunication for opposing Cardinal Wolsey's reforms. During 1531 the Observants further incurred Henry VIII's displeasure through their determined opposition to his divorce and Forest seems to have almost gone out of his way to attract the king's wrath. In November 1532 Forest preached at St Paul's cross, one of the most notable pulpits in England, railing against the moral decay of the realm and the destruction of the churches. At the beginning of February 1533 an attempt at reconciliation was made between him and Henry, but a few months later he fled London, where it was becoming clear that he was no longer safe. This did not keep him from trouble for long and he seems to have already been in Newgate prison in 1534, most likely due to the consequences of the king's total suppression of the Observants in that year, during which over 200 of the friars were imprisoned, some in common jails and some in houses of other Franciscans and Augustinians. During his imprisonment Forest corresponded with the queen and wrote a treatise against Henry's assumption of the headship of the English Church. On 8 April 1538, Forest was taken to Lambeth, where he was ordered to make an act of abjuration. Forest refused with no apparent hesitation and was instead sentenced to burn as a heretic. On 22 May he was taken to Smithfield to be burned. Forest's martyrdom was said to have lasted a full two hours, after which he was given a heretic's burial.

Forest's execution on 22 May is marked by a peculiar story: it seems that in the preparations for his execution, a wooden statue of a particular Welsh saint had been brought to London from North Wales. This wooden statue, that of St Derfel Gadarn, had itself been the subject of a prophecy, in which it was said that it would one day burn down a forest. A contemporary inscription, according to some sources nailed above Forest's gallows, tells some of the story:

David Darvell Gatheren,
As saith the Welshmen,
Fetched outlaws out of hell;
Now is he come with spere and shilde
In harness to burn at Smithfield,
For in Wales he may not dwell.
And Forest the Friar,
That obstinate liar,
That wilfullie shall be dead,
In his contumacie
The gospell doth denie
The king to be supreme head.

Whether the prophecy existed before the burning of John Forest, or whether it was invented to provide a sense of religious theatricality for the execution, is a matter for debate, but the grim gallows humour of the English Reformation is readily apparent. Derfel Gadarn, or Cadarn, the Mighty, was associated with the parish church at Llandderfel, east of Bala in north Wales; this church still exists and displays with its porch a remnant of the medieval statue of Derfel. Derfel was also said to have been an abbot at Bardsey Isle, a monastic foundation also associated with St Dubric, the man who, according to Geoffrey of Monmouth, performed Arthur's marriage to Guinevere.

The wooden statue of Derfel Gadarn had only recently arrived in London. In early April, the Commissary for the diocese of St Asaph had come to Llandderfel and sent back a report. Elis Price wrote that the parish had an image of the saint, 'in whome the people have so greate confidence, hope and truste that they cumme dayly a pilgrimage unto hym' offering gifts of cattle, horses or money. Price's presence in Llandderfel on the day following Derfel's feast day is probably not a coincidence, as he and his master Thomas Cromwell were diligent in their pursuit of the evils of Catholic superstition and of whatever profits they could earn from that pursuit. Cromwell ordered the statue to be confiscated and sent to London and despite the priest and parishioners offering Price £40 to save the icon it was dispatched by the end of the month. Along with the statue, Price sent a warning to the extent that the parishioners were planning to follow it and make an official complaint concerning his behaviour. Whatever became of the delegation is unknown, but if it did travel to London then it clearly did not meet with any great success. A second statue of Derfel, this time taken from a smaller shrine at Llanfihangel Llantarnam, is also said to have made the journey to England and to have met the same fiery fate.

Price testifies to the local belief that Derfel could fetch damned souls out of Hell, a spiritual impossibility according to the tenets of medieval Christian theology, but which nonetheless appears to have been part of his cult. It perhaps may be argued that Derfel's intervention was thought to be able to assist those souls still passing through Purgatory, a state halfway between Heaven and Hell where souls were purified and made worthy of eventual admission to Paradise. Welsh Arthurian legend, however, tells a marvellous story in which Arthur and his men sought to capture a miraculous cauldron, in which the dead could be revived, from the Otherworld realm of Annwn. According to the bard Taliesin who relates the story, only seven of Arthur's men, including

5 The surviving remains of the medieval statue of St Derfel Gadarn,
now housed in the porch of his church at Llandderfel. *Courtesy of A5
Publications*

Taliesin himself, survive the voyage. Another Welsh text, *Culwch and
Olwen*, later transforms this early tale and records a similar journey, in
which the prize that Arthur and his knights pursue becomes a more
prosaic cauldron full of Irish coins. The story of Arthur's pursuit of a
magical cauldron which is associated with life-giving properties – a
story that is argued by some critics to lie behind the story of the Holy
Grail itself – hints at possible connections between the Arthurian legends, particular characters and the motif of rescue from the Otherworld,
which is transformed by sixteenth-century believers to be Hell, from
which Arthur's knight Derfel can save them through his holy power.

We unfortunately have no surviving medieval *Life of St Derfel*, but
other medieval sources inform us of his strong Arthurian connections.
Unlike the majority of other saints' *Vitae* mentioned above, the stories
of Derfel and Arthur do not seem to be centred around conflict over
the rights of the local church. Their exact relationship is unknown, but
Elissa Henken has traced 46 distinct references to Derfel within Welsh
medieval poetry, which often praises his ability in battle and associates

him with the Arthurian court. Derfel is further said to have been one
of seven survivors of Camlan, Arthur's last battle:

> Here are the names of the men who escaped from the battle of
> Camlan: Sandde Angel's form because of his beauty, Morfran son
> of Tegid because of his ugliness, St Cynfelyn from the speed of his
> horse, St Pedrog from the strength of his spear, Derfel the Strong
> from his strength, Geneid the Tall from his speed.

This list, found in a manuscript of Evan Evans, is the most complete in
that it names all seven of the survivors; that five of the seven are known
saints might indicate that survival at Camlann is a traditional British
method of honouring a saint.

Of the four saintly survivors of Camlann, we know the most about
Pedrog, a little more about Derfel, and very little indeed about either
Cynfelyn or Cedwyn. Pedrog, who survived Camlann 'by the strength
of his spear', also took up the holy life. His martial prowess, like Derfel's,
is widely attested: he was known in the Triads as one of the Three
Just Knights of Arthur's Court, Pedrog Splintered-Spear, son of Prince
Clement of Cornwall. He is also sometimes said to be the son of a
Welsh king and the uncle of St Cadoc (who may have died in battle
against the Saxons). Numerous poems utilise Pedrog as the very image
of the spear-wielding warrior and he could sometimes be confused with
Peredur of the Long Spear, the Welsh Perceval. Pedrog was known to
have shot a single spear through seven men and his primary relic was,
unsurprisingly, a spear held by his church at Llanbedrog, where Sir Lewis
Newburgh saw it in 1535. Other, more traditional relics of Pedrog could
be found at Exeter Cathedral and at Bodmin, although the latter relics
were stolen in 1177 and taken to Saint-Méen in Brittany, before the
English King Henry II secured their return after the Prior of Bodmin
complained about the theft.

As we have seen, Derfel's statue was not so fortunate as the Bodmin
relics of Pedrog, but a remnant of the medieval statue of Derfel still
survives today despite the ravages of time and religious conflict. The
remnant has been the subject of a variety of interpretations, in large
part because it is in such bad shape: not only did Price play his part
in the statue's destruction, but he was followed by a local Dean who

ordered the animal decapitated in 1730, after which it was used as an playground ride by local children every Easter Tuesday. The remaining wooden piece seems to be the torso of an animal, sometimes said to be a horse and sometimes to be a red stag. One observer, the eighteenth-century Welsh artist Edward Pugh, imagined it to be a red lion. As Baring-Gould noted, 'Stag or steed, it has suffered very much.' But all observers agree that it was life-sized and that it was mobile: the neck could be moved in its socket and in the back of the image there still exists a square cavity in which the image of Derfel was probably placed. William Eist, in 1898, reported the image had a mechanism by which Derfel's eyes opened and closed and the limbs moved; this late report is perhaps suspect, but as seen above there is some evidence for the image's mechanical nature. Still visible on the remains today are faint traces of red paint, pointing to the fact that the medieval statue, like all medieval art, would have been painted and decorated in the rich vibrant style of contemporary churches. The figure of Derfel himself was reported to have been carved wearing full armour rather than ecclesiastical garb, pointing to his origins as a warrior. The saint was also said to have been holding some type of spear or walking staff. Another chapel dedicated to Derfel at Llanfihangel Llantarnam in Monmouthshire had a relic, but the nature of this object is unknown; it might well be nothing other than the second statue mentioned above.

The possibility that the animal associated with Derfel was a red stag is intriguing. Many British saints, especially in Wales and Ireland, are associated with stags. Derfel's apprentice Illtud, discussed above, acquired the services of a strange creature: he witnessed a stag and a horse mating and the resulting offspring was a hybrid creature that was noted for its speed. Illtud also had a tame stag come to him for sanctuary and, when saved, it gratefully stayed to assist the saint with his chores; another story mentions a golden stag belonging to Illtud which is buried near the tiny village of Llantwit Major, which will be restored to prominence when the stag is found. This same story of a helpful stag is told of Saints David (patron saint of Wales), Cadog, Teilo and others. The motif of the hunted stag is not simply meant to indicate a saint's compassion; the fleeing stag can also mystically mark the boundaries of a saint's land, the future site of his church. The story of St Oudoceus is typical of this motif: King Einion of Glewyssig and his men are hunting a stag, which flees to Oudoceus for protection. The huntsmen find the exhausted animal lying at the saint's feet and the king begs the saint's pardon, giving the stag and all the land around which it ran to Oudoceus.

Some such story may lie behind Derfel's animal companion, if it is in fact a stag. That Derfel appears to have ridden the animal is not necessarily a sign that it was a horse; Illtud's half-horse, half-deer creature might have influenced the Derfel story, providing him with a mystical steed. There are signs that Derfel's cult might be a late one, more influenced by than influencing the other *Lives* of his fellow saints. His survival at Camlann seems to be an authentic tradition, but what emphasis should be placed on the failure of the source to call him a 'saint' is unknown and the lack of a surviving written *Life* hampers any attempt at understanding Derfel's cult. It may be that Pedrog was associated with Camlann after Derfel, but local traditions in Merionethshire soon insisted that Derfel, too, was a saint.

The statue's importance to the local community at Llandderfel is obvious from Price's own account, but also from this brief discussion of the British saints and their influence. The Welsh tradition of the 20,000 Saints of Bardsey Island (Ynys Enlli) reminds us of the interconnected nature of the British saints: most of the Bardsey saints are unnamed, but Derfel is sometimes said to have been an abbot on the island. The entire landscapes of Wales and Cornwall are infused with the memory of their saints: Llandderfel means 'St Derfel's' just as Llanbedrog means 'St Pedrog's' and Llantwit means 'St Illtud's'. The village derived its very identity from the saint and his church. There are very few similar place-names in England: only St Albans and Bury St Edmund, perhaps, come immediately to mind. That the average Arthurian enthusiast in modern times ignores the Welsh saints except when they come into direct contact with Arthur is unfortunate, but the secular English legend of Arthur has been so successful in imprinting itself onto both the popular mind and the very landscape that there is little room for more authentic native traditions. The manner in which the Cornish, in particular, tried to fight or accommodate themselves to this international tidal wave needs to be examined.

TINTAGEL: A FANTASY CASTLE

Tintagel Castle is well known as the legendary birthplace of Arthur, but as Henry Jenner noted, we know very little about its true history. Jenner made this remark in 1926, in a speech given at Tintagel itself during a round of archaeological digs, yet we know little more of substance now than we did then. The site seems to have been inhabited at some point after the withdrawal of Roman troops from Britain and was apparently a site of trade with the Mediterranean world. The surrounding area, known as Botcinnii (now Bossiney), appears in the Domesday Book, but no castle is mentioned as standing on the narrow headland. The first we hear of a castle on Tintagel itself is in the *History* of Geoffrey of Monmouth, where it is the location of a great stronghold under the control of Gorlois, the Duke of Cornwall. Geoffrey finishes his book around 1136 and it was around this time that we see the first signs of Tintagel's growing significance as a place of import: one Henry Fitzcount, who administered the Earldom of Cornwall on behalf of King John, granted the castle to Gervase de Hornacot, who immediately changed his name to Gervase de Tintagel. It is therefore not surprising that the Cornish are treated kindly by Geoffrey; they are the descendants of Corineus, a Trojan companion of the British founder Brutus, and his descendants frequently come to rule the entire island whenever the British royal family destroys itself through fratricide (a frequent occurrence in the *History*). At some point between the Domesday Book in 1086 and Geoffrey's *History*, somebody (possibly Reginald, brother of Robert of Gloucester, one of Geoffrey's patrons) constructs a castle at Tintagel and this castle becomes known as the place where Arthur was conceived. It is interesting to note that it is not until the fifteenth century that the castle also becomes the site of Arthur's birth: William of Worcester appears to be the first writer to make the connection in 1478.

The family of de Hornacot only held the castle until 1233. Richard, a brother of Henry III, had been given the Earldom of Cornwall in 1227, the year after having lost possession of Poitou in France. As an outsider Richard may have felt the need to ingratiate himself with his Cornish subjects. Cornwall, although no longer widely considered one of the British nations alongside England, Wales, Scotland and Ireland, maintained a strong sense of independence throughout the Middle Ages and it was only following Henry VII's victory at Bosworth Field that Cornish culture began to be fully absorbed into the English nation. In 1235 the Cornish could still view their new earl, the king's brother, as a foreign interloper – and although Cornish rebellions never met with any great success, they were nonetheless common occurrences. The earl had a great deal to lose should he experience trouble in his new lands: the Cornish tin mines were a source of substantial wealth, as they had been since antiquity but increasingly since King John had instituted the Stanneries, royal institutions which granted Cornish tin miners a surprising degree of autonomy and self-regulation. Furthermore, in addition to his interests in strengthening his hold over Cornwall, Richard also had wider ambitions within England and, indeed, across continental Europe. The legendary significance of the castle at Tintagel must have seemed like a goldmine of symbolic potential for an ambitious noble like Richard.

Richard lost no time in obtaining the estates around Tintagel, acquiring them at no little cost from the de Hornacot family. Once he had possession of the lands he rebuilt much of the castle, producing the bulk of that still standing on the site today. It seems likely that Richard's interest in Tintagel was very much of an antiquarian and symbolic nature. There would have been little practical reason for Richard to rebuild the castle at such great expense. The location had little strategic purpose and it was expensive to build, maintain and provision: the headland itself was not ideal for the kind of grand-scale building Richard intended. Major engineering was required to level the land and the castle itself seemed to hang from the cliffs. The castle was built in an antiquated style, with none of the modern features Richard that incorporated into the castle that he rebuilt at nearby Launceston. Richard was the Earl of Cornwall and presenting himself as the heir to Arthur in 'a ready made fantasy castle' seems to have been much more about his image than any practical need. His legendary ambitions could not be any plainer and what's more, they seem to have worked.

Apparently the wealthiest and most influential magnate in England, due largely to his control of the tin trade and his policy of lending money to fellow nobles, he refused the crown of Sicily in 1252 when it was offered by Pope Innocent IV; Richard was instead saving himself

6 Golant Church, near Fowey in Cornwall, where Isolde's robe was treasured as a relic during the Middle Ages

for higher things. His brother-in-law Frederick II was the Holy Roman Emperor, ruler of Germany, and Richard had high hopes of being named as his successor. In 1256, while still in Cornwall, this personal dream came true and he was named 'King of the Romans'. Although Richard pursued the imperial crown until 1269, he was never formally named Emperor by the Pope and the Empire proved a great drain on his resources. In the meantime, his policy at home vacillated between loyalty to his brother Henry III and outright rebellion. Most notably, Richard briefly flirted with joining the famous rebellion of Simon de Montfort, but was soon convinced to rejoin the royal cause. After Richard died in 1272, the castle at Tintagel gradually fell into disrepair, despite later belonging to the Black Prince, son of Arthurian enthusiast Edward III, in the mid-fourteenth century.

Richard's rebuilding of the castle at Tintagel made it into much more than just a place: it became a conscious historical statement about Arthur, about Cornwall, about Richard himself. Just as much as Edward I's table helped to fix Winchester as an Arthurian site and, eventually, as Camelot itself, the walls of Richard's Tintagel Castle were now the very walls that had witnessed the machinations of Merlin and the conception of Arthur. In trying to associate himself with the aura of King Arthur, Richard helped to firmly fix one Arthurian story to a specific historical place despite contrary trends within the legends themselves.

Prior to Richard's involvement and to some extent afterwards, Tintagel was also strongly associated with another strand of the Arthurian legend, the previously unrelated story of the lovers Tristan and Isolde. In Malory's *Morte Darthur*, the role of Tintagel is often a confused one, where it is depicted as the home of the villainous King Mark of Cornwall. Nowhere in Malory is it stated that Mark is related to Arthur or Gorlois, or that Cornwall seems to have had a duke (Cador) as well as a king. Malory tells all these stories quite happily, even though they at times contradict each other. In the earliest forms of the Tristan narrative Tintagel is not the setting of the story, and in one of these tales we find another famous Arthurian object: the so-called dress of Isolde, wife of King Mark and the lover of his nephew Tristan.

A GARMENT WORTH A HUNDRED SILVER MARKS

In the twelfth-century French *Tristan,* written by Béroul, we are told that King Mark resides at a place called Lancien, which has been identified as Lantine in Golant (near Fowey on the south coast of Cornwall). Béroul tells us another story associated with Golant, which provides us with a historically attested but very unusual Arthurian relic. The church of St Samson at Golant claims to have once possessed a cloth of rich silk embroidered in silk and gold thread that was said to have been offered to the church by Isolde, the queen of Cornwall. During one of the periods of reconciliation between Mark and Isolde, the queen makes an offering to the church of St Samson:

> They went along the main road up to the church of St Samson. The queen [Isolde] went there together with all the barons. The bishop came out to meet her with his clerks, monks and abbots, all wearing albs and copes. The queen dismounted and put on a dark blue cloak. The bishop took her hand and conducted her into the church and

up to the altar. The brave Dinas, a fine baron, brought her a garment worth fully a hundred silver marks, made of silk richly embroidered with gold: no count or king ever had such a garment. Queen Yseut took it and with a good heart laid it on the altar. It was afterwards made into a chasuble, which only leaves the church treasury on great annual feasts. Those who have seen it say it is still in St Samson's.

Isolde's temporary reconciliation with her husband Mark is symbolised by a gift to a local church, an act that makes the reconciliation itself a vow before God.

It is not known whether the church of St Samson at Golant really had such a relic when Béroul likely visited the region in the twelfth century: he makes no claims to have seen the chasuble for himself. Samson is yet another Celtic saint who is associated, although indirectly, with Arthur: he is said to have studied under the learned St Illtud at the latter's monastery at Llanwit in Glamorgan. Samson became involved in Breton and Frankish politics late in life and apparently became the Bishop of Dol in Brittany at the behest of King Childebert of the Franks. Samson yet again reminds us that the Welsh, Bretons and Cornish of the fifth and sixth centuries were part of a wide interconnected Celtic world, intricately linked with each other and to the growing Arthurian legend. The current church at Golant was consecrated in 1509, over three centuries after Béroul wrote his poem, although parts of the church date from the earlier thirteenth century. What *is* known is that, soon after Béroul's text appeared, the presence of Isolde's cloth is testified to by other sources.

Béroul claims that the church displayed the chasuble, a long sleeveless robe worn by a priest who is officiating over a Mass, only at an annual feast and thus it does not seem to have been in regular use as a vestment. If, as some scholars believe, Béroul created the story whole-cloth, then it might be argued that the priests of St Samson recognised a good thing when they heard it and simply claimed that a chasuble already in their possession was the ancient robe of Isolde. It might strike a modern reader as odd that a church would be so eager to claim a vestment made from cloth offered by an adulteress who, after all that was said and done, continued her adultery after the moment of reconciliation. However, given the prestige associated with the Arthurian objects that we have seen thus far, we can perhaps understand the attraction. Furthermore, a great deal of the chasuble's symbolic importance must come from its royal connection: even if the Lancien area had not been the home of a powerful Cornish monarch, it remained true that the legend of Tristan and Isolde spoke of a time of Cornish independence and, in Béroul at least, lordship over all of England. The church of St Samson thus subtly links itself with strong memories of Cornish power. Here again, as with the statue of Derfel Gadarn, we find a local significance being placed upon an item that participates in the construction of a powerful sense of regional identity, again illustrating the flexibility of the Arthurian legends in terms of their political and ideological use.

ADULTERY REVISITED: CRADDOCK'S MANTLE

Isolde's robe is not the only item of clothing that was claimed to have survived from Arthur's time. We find another relic of the Arthurian past that links chasubles and adultery in another Arthurian story, that of Craddok's mantle. As we have seen in chapter 3, Caxton tells us that Craddok's mantle could be seen at Dover beside Gawain's skull (a story repeated by Robert Chester in his 1601 anthology *Love's Martyr*). This mantle has sometimes been associated with a character from the militaristic poem, the *Alliterative Morte Arthure*. Arthur, conquering Europe and about to descend upon Rome, meets a pilgrim bearing a message:

> At the rising of the sun he [Arthur] see coming,
> Going towards Rome by the quickest route,
> A man in a round cloak with very roomy clothes
> And a hat with comfortable shoes homely and round …

This man, named Craddok, was once a knight of Arthur's court, but had been driven out of England by Mordred's rebellion; he and Arthur do not recognise each other, but Arthur takes the message to heart and turns for home, where he will face Mordred in the final battle. The association of Dover with both Gawain's skull and Craddock's mantle perhaps suggests that the alliterative poem was the inspiration for the items at Dover. Yet the tradition of infidelity associated with the mantle is the more powerful one. The mantle, which we remember would magically shrink if placed upon the shoulders of an unfaithful wife, is located by Thomas Gray at Glastonbury. It may be that the Béroul story is influencing Gray and other writers who tell the Glastonbury story, but the link between Arthurian holy sites, priestly vestments and reconciled adultery is suggestive. Was it meant, perhaps, to hint at the mercy of God and the church, extended even to famous adulterers like Tristan and Isolde, or Lancelot and Guinevere (who, after all, end their lives as a holy hermit and an abbess respectively)?

NOT WANTED IN THE TRADITION

The objects discussed in this chapter are in many cases actual relics in the traditional religious meaning of the term. Many of these objects were geographically and culturally marginal: a saint such as Derfel, however interesting, was not going to take the literary world by storm from his distant Merionethshire stronghold. Similarly, while the church at Golant found ways to earn money and prestige from Béroul's story of Isolde's donation, subsequent adaptors and translators had little interest in the tiny church on the southern coast of Cornwall. There may well have been ancient connections between the Tristan story, Lancien and Golant, but later writers looked towards Richard's magnificent castle at Tintagel and simply relocated the entire story. While Henry II could be convinced to intervene on Bodmin Priory's behalf when Pedrog's relics were stolen in the twelfth century, a later Henry would ultimately be responsible for theft of the relics and destruction on a massive scale. The statue – or possibly statues – of Derfel Gadarn joined other famous Arthurian objects on the Tudor scrap heap, along with Arthur's royal seal at Westminster and his black marble tomb at Glastonbury. It is no coincidence that Glastonbury always appeared to be in some sense connected to the Celtic world, despite its location in Anglo-Saxon Somerset.

In the Celtic world, resistance always co-existed with assimilation. Many of the troops who faced Llywelyn's armies were Welsh themselves, but the Welsh story of resistance and aspiration is better known than the parallel narrative that took place in Cornwall. In part, the Welsh manage to put themselves on the national radar far more effectively; Owain

Glendower appears in Shakespeare's *Henry IV*, after all, a claim that cannot be made for any native Cornishman. Henry VII derived some of his authority from his Welsh ancestry, which related him to Arthur and other British princes. However, we must also keep in mind that the Welsh March lasted into the late Middle Ages and increasing survival rates for documentation ensured that we simply know more about the Welsh than we do about the Cornish, whose resistance effectively ended in the eleventh century. The Cornish, despite being considered a separate people within the wider kingdom as late at the fifteenth century, became honorary Englishmen and their land an English holiday destination: safe, atmospheric but not alarmingly so, and with access to beaches.

The Cornish saw their traditional rights eroded by the Tudors, a not-uncommon experience as the English monarchy accelerated the process of centralisation and Anglicisation of the island. The Cornish language was on a permanent defensive, dying out entirely as a living language in the twentieth century; Cornish efforts to resist the English Prayer Book in 1549 and Cornish loyalty to the Royalist cause of Charles I further damaged Cornwall's status. A series of rebellions marked Cornwall's entry into the early modern world: 1497, 1548-49, 1642 and 1648 all saw significant Cornish insurrection. Cornwall provided the bulk of the troops for Perkin Warbeck's supremely unsuccessful rebellion against Henry VII. The Cornish were eventually broken and even their belief in the return of Arthur, once so strong as to inspire a group of villagers in Bodmin to attack a group of sceptical French monks, became associated with the English other.

Tintagel plays an important role in this process: the castle may be seen by the romantically inclined as the place where Arthur was born, but in reality it is the place where Geoffrey of Monmouth, servant of the English king, said Arthur was born. The brother and uncle of later English kings, Richard 'of Cornwall', agreed; it is largely the remains of the castle that he built, perched as it is on the side of the cliff, that we visit today. Tintagel is an integral part of the Arthurian legend because the English decided that it should be so. When the villainous Mark becomes the lord of Tintagel in the Prose *Tristan*, a massive cycle of stories focusing on Tristran's chivalry rather than his love for Isolde, he is accompanied by his Cornish followers. Cowardly and treacherous, these are the Cornish who appear in Malory's *Morte Darthur.* Arthur's knights Kay, Brandiles, Tor and Sagremor all agree that good knights never come from Cornwall, while Dinadan openly accuses Cornish knights of 'cowardyse' as a general trait. Lancelot's half-brother Ector de Maris openly laments for his reputation after he has been defeated by Tristram, who is disguised as an unknown Cornish knight. How much this has to do with the Cornish reputation for rebellion is unknown, but villainous Cornish knights are commonplace in non-Arthurian medieval romances as well. Long past were the days when Geoffrey's heroic Cornishmen, Arthur included, had often come to save the day for the British.

The Welsh and Cornish sought to preserve the memory of Arthur as their own particular heritage. Welsh saints fight at Camlann or against the Saxons more directly. Cornish churches preserve the memory of a native royal house, one that was increasingly denigrated in texts coming from the dominant English and continental culture. Welsh translations of Geoffrey of Monmouth eliminate references to the final defeat of the British, or translate the names of prominent characters back into versions more familiar to them: Peredur for Perceval, Gwalchmai for Gawain. Resistance on the level of the text, like armed resistance in the field, never quite comes to an end even when the Arthurian tradition seems entirely dominated by the English. When Steven Spielberg decided to film a new Arthurian television series in Cornwall, the Welsh Legislative Assembly lodged a formal protest: Arthur was Welsh and everybody ought to know that. What the Welsh argument says about the possibility of a renewed Cornish nation is better left for another time and place.

St Illtud has a possible connection with Tintagel, which is both tenuous and suggestive. It has been argued that the late eleventh-century chapel on the headland above the castle, dedicated to St Juliot, is in fact a chapel to Illtud. Whether the chapel was built on the site of an older sacred building is still debated and obviously the patron saint of any previous structure is unknowable. The possible rationale for building the chapel in such an isolated position, when the town already had a church, is also unclear. However, Leland records the name of the chapel's patron saint as Ulitte, which is ambiguous and could well represent the name Illtud instead. Unfortunately, there are few churches dedicated to Illtud in Cornwall, although he was very popular in Wales. The one known Cornish site is St Dominick just west of the River Tamar, where an Illtud chapel once existed. If Richard really was sufficiently interested in the Arthurian legend to rebuild Tintagel Castle, then is it not within the realms of possibility that he might also have built a chapel dedicated to Illtud or, if we assume that he only had access to the mainstream tradition descended from Geoffrey of Monmouth, one dedicated to Dubricius?

It would seem not. Juliot, or Julitta, is a saint associated with Tarsus in Asia Minor and her cult seems to have absorbed a few local saints with similar names. Churches dedicated to her appear throughout north Cornwall. Catherine Rachel John is not certain of Juliot's patronage of the chapel at Tintagel, for which there seems to be little proof, and in her entry for Juliot in *The Saints of Cornwall*, she primarily dwells upon Tintagel's Arthurian connections. The question of the Tintagel dedication remains an open one, but the weight of circumstantial evidence seems to militate against any Arthurian surprises.

The English were passionate in their interest in the imperial Arthur, as we have seen time and again in this book. Their Arthur was a conqueror, not a defender, and the English were generally less interested in his wars against their ancestors the Saxons than in his civil wars: wars against rebellious kings in Scotland, Wales, Ireland and Cornwall. Malory may argue that the Cornish were wretched knights, but his book includes a mention of the 'marchis of Cornuwayle', a heavily militarised but fictional area of conflict between England and the southwest peninsula that mirrored those found on the borders with Wales and Scotland. The English Arthurian tradition was one that was largely concerned with imperial domination, especially as it was used by Edward I. The Great Seal at Westminster, after all, listed Arthur's many imperial conquests but never once mentioned the Round Table, and nor did it mention Wales, Cornwall or Scotland, only the imperial unity of Britain.

7

Desiring Arthur

Pierre Nora has described how memorials, statues and other monuments operate as *lieux de memoire*, places of memory, providing physical and visual texts that narrate the official history of a nation or a people. In this book we have tried to demonstrate how the Arthurian artefacts and relics of the medieval period were intended to perform a similar role: they function in this sense as portable places, sites of pilgrimage in the popular devotion to the Arthurian past. In a predominantly illiterate society, these objects spoke with a simple and clear eloquence to their varied audience. The creation of these relics is intertwined with the medieval desire to 'make real' the past. The artefacts that were fabricated by the medieval kings, nobles and monks represent the manifestation of a wide range of cultural and political purposes illustrate the willingness of the medieval mind to believe in the historicity of the legends of Arthur. Without the widespread belief in the historical truth of the legends, a belief due in large part to the writings of Geoffrey of Monmouth and those writers who further developed his *History* in their own later chronicles, these relics would never have been created. Underpinning their utility and authenticity within medieval society was the authority of the written word, highlighting the importance of both Arthurian literature and chronicle within medieval culture.

We have seen how the Arthurian relics of English royal or monastic origin seek to draw the reputation of Arthur towards the centre, thus reconstructing Arthur as a safe, stable and, most importantly, English figure. The politically motivated transferral of Arthur's seal and crown to the shrine of St Edward in Westminster Abbey, the construction of the Round Table at Winchester, and the discovery of Arthur's grave at Glastonbury all point towards a powerful and consistent attempt to appropriate Arthur as an English hero, an attempt to erase his former identity as a leader of the Celts against the forebears of the English. Conversely, we see in the Celtic Arthurian relics a stubborn reminder of Arthur's legendary past, locating his legends at the very margins of the English state. These Celtic objects resist the pull towards the cultural and institutional centre, and seek to retain Arthur as a hero of the dispossessed Celtic Britons. They are also an indication of the narrative instability of the Arthurian tradition as a whole.

Of course, not everyone in the medieval period took these relics seriously. There were doubters of the Arthurian legends, and even amongst the firm believers there were ongoing debates over the location and authenticity of some of the objects. The 'many evydences' that Caxton points to as proof of the existence of Arthur represent only one set of stories, privileging those locations that were in vogue during the late fifteenth century. Prior to this time, items such as Craddok's mantle and Gawain's remains are associated with various different sites, pointing towards a dynamic atmosphere of competition for the various aspects of Arthur's legacy.

While the relics in this book are the product of a medieval belief in the reality of the Arthurian legends, this desire to find evidence of Arthur's existence does not seem to have been extinguished by the arrival of the modern era. The desire to touch the past, to make contact with the supposed historicity of Arthur in a very real and tangible sense, is still with us, and the search for Arthurian artefacts continues. The quest for the historical Arthur has consumed a vast quantity of paper throughout the last century, and has involved numerous claims and counterclaims, interspersed with 'amazing' discoveries, which inevitably turn out to disappoint. An illuminating example of the way in which this modern desire for Arthur operates can be seen in the discovery of the 'Artognou' stone on the headland at Tintagel. This fragment of Roman stone, uncovered during an archaeological dig in the summer of 1998, was found have a sixth-century inscription that was interpreted as reading 'PATER COLIAVI FICIT ARTOGNOU' (Artognou, father of a descendant of Coll, has had this made). Despite the reservations of the archaeologists involved in the dig, the news was soon out. The national press, ever in the mood for a sensational story, ran with head-lines that this was 'proof' that a Dark Age King Arthur really had lived and ruled at Tintagel. More surprisingly, English Heritage also got in on the act, releasing a press statement entitled 'Arthur: is this where myth meets history?'. Despite the fact that, even on onomastic grounds alone, the inscription has nothing at all to say about anyone named Arthur, the latent cultural desire to connect with the Arthurian past spurred on both newsmen and heritage professionals alike. One might even take a pause for a moment to consider whether the motivations of English Heritage in this case were so different from those of the Glastonbury monks in 1191?

Such examples of Arthur-mania reveal the continued presence of the medieval desire for the discovery of artefacts that will somehow 'prove' the existence of a historical Arthur. Jeffrey Jerome Cohen, the American cultural critic *par excellence*, has commented on the futility of the modern desire to locate Arthur within the bounds of known history:

> Despite the frantic search for a historical Arthur exemplified by Henry II and the Glastonbury monks, and which even now animates scholars like Geoffrey Ashe, the veridicality of the king's existence is ultimately beside the point.

Of course, in one sense, Cohen is completely right. The place where Arthur truly sleeps remains within the realms of the imagination, where he waits with his knights, ready to ride forth whenever there is a new idea that he can champion. The ongoing search for a historical Arthur is highly unlikely to throw much light upon his deep-seated importance within Western European culture and history. But, from another stand-point, the fact that during the medieval period Arthur was considered to be real *is* important, and to comprehend the lasting power of this search for Arthur's historicity, and the way in which this desire for Arthur was utilised in the medieval period, is to peer into the work-ings of the medieval mind. In the Middle Ages the historically attested

Arthur represented many things to many people, just as he does today. To the Celtic peoples he was a saviour in waiting; to the Glastonbury monks he was a valuable marketing tool; and to the English kings he was symbolic of their imperial ambitions to rule across the whole of the British Isles. The historicity of Arthur did matter, and the sheer number and variety of medieval relics that we have examined in this study stand testament to this fact.

Further reading

Primary sources include Sir Thomas Malory's *Morte Darthur*, from *Works*, edited by Eugène Vinaver, 1 volume (Oxford, 1971); Geoffrey of Monmouth, *The History of the Kings of Britain*, ed. Lewis Thorpe (Penguin, 1966); *The Death of Arthur*, ed. James Cable (Penguin, 1971), is the most easily accessible version of the French *Mort Artu*; the Awntyrs of Arthur can be found in Thomas Hahn, *Sir Gawain: Eleven Romances and Tales* (TEAMS, 1995); the *Alliterative Morte Arthure*, from *King Arthur's Death*, ed. Larry Benson (TEAMS, 1994). Some reference has been made to *The Mabinogion*, translated by Gwyn Jones and Thomas Jones (Everyman, 1993).

CHAPTER I

On the medieval cult of relics, please see Patrick Geary, *Furta Sacra*, revised edition (Princeton, 1990) and *Living With the Dead in the Middle Ages* (Cornell University, 1994); on modern versions of the relic cult, see Angela Jane Weisl, *The Persistence of Medievalism* (Palgrave MacMillan, 2003). On specifically Arthurian relics, see the two articles by E.M.R. Ditmas, 'The Cult of Arthurian Relics', *Folklore* 75 (1964), pp. 19-33, and 'More Arthurian Relics', *Folklore* 77 (1966), pp. 91-104. Christopher Dean also discusses many of these objects in *Arthur of England* (Toronto,

1987), especially in chapter 3, 'Arthur and the Common Folk', but reaches very different conclusions than the present authors. The interested reader will also find some (very literary) discussion of the Arthurian legend in England in Richard J. Moll, *Before Malory: Reading Arthur in Later Medieval England* (University of Toronto, 2004). On the art of and motivations for medieval forgeries of all kinds, Alfred Hiatt, *The Making of Medieval Forgeries* (British Library, 2004).

CHAPTER 2

On the science and history of the Round Table at Winchester, please see Martin Biddle, ed. *King Arthur's Round Table* (Boydell, 2000); on the legendary history of Winchester in general, Robert Rouse, *The Idea of the Anglo-Saxon England in Middle English Romance* (D.S. Brewer, 2005), especially chapter 6. The standard biography of Edward I, whose life and reign is of fundamental importance to the present book, is Michael Prestwich, *Edward I*, 2nd edition (Yale University Press, 1997). Prestwich is sceptical of Edward's reputation for Arthurianism, suggesting that the king was interested in chivalric stories in general; R.S. Loomis published the influential article that started this trend, 'Edward I, Arthurian Enthusiast', *Speculum* 28 (1953), pp. 114-27. For the idea of human skin on church doors, both here concerning the Danes but with possible reference to the 1303 robbery discussed in chapter 4, please see M.J. Swanton, 'Dane-Skins: Excoriation in Early England', in *Folklore* 87 (1976), 21-28.

CHAPTER 3

Many of the sources on Arthurian Glastonbury are collected in James P. Carley, ed. *Glastonbury Abbey and the Arthurian Tradition* (D.S. Brewer, 2001). Michael Wood usefully examines the role of Glastonbury in both English history and identity in chapters 3 and 4 of his *In Search of England* (Penguin, 2000), while the role of Arthur more generally in medieval society and politics is addressed by Carley in his 'Arthur in English History', in *The Arthur of the English*, ed. by W.R.J. Barron (University of Wales, 2001). The story of Perkin Warbeck has most recently been told by Ann Wroe, *Perkin: A Story of Deception* (Jonathon Cape, 2003).

CHAPTER 4

On Gaveston, see Pierre Chaplais, *Piers Gaveston: Edward II's Adoptive Brother* (Clarendon Press, 1994); but also see J.S. Hamilton's response in 'Ménage à Roi: Edward II and Piers Gaveston', in *History Today* 49.6 (1999), pp. 26-31. On Gaveston's alleged thefts, again see Hamilton, 'Piers Gaveston and the Royal Treasure', in *Albion* 23 (1991), pp. 201-207. On the cults of the political saints, see Simon Walker, 'Political Saints in Later England', *The MacFarlane Legacy: Studies in Late Medieval Politics and Society*, ed. Richard H. Britnell and Anthony J. Pollard (Palgrave McFarlane, 1995); for Henry VI in particular, Leigh Ann Craig has begun to examine the Henry cult in detail: 'Royalty, Virtue, and Adversity: The Cult of Henry VI', in *Albion* 35 (2003), pp. 187-209.

CHAPTER 5

John Julius Norwich, *Kingdom of the Sun, 1130-94* (Longman, 1970), is a good, general introduction to the history of Sicily. On Tristram and Curtana, see R.S. Loomis, 'Vestiges of Tristram in London', *Burlington Magazine* 41 (1922), p. 59, and more accessibly, 'Tristram and the House of Anjou', *Modern Languages Review* 17 (1922), pp. 24-30. The Scrope-Grosvenor controversy has been much discussed, including Ronald Stewart-Brown, 'The Scrope and Grosvenor Controversy, 1385-91', *Transactions of the Historic Society of Lancashire and Chesire* 89 (1937), pp. 1-22; and Lee Patterson, *Chaucer and the Subject of History* (Routledge, 1991), especially pp. 179-89. On Cambridge and Arthur, see Ad Putter, 'King Arthur at Oxbridge: Nicholas Cantelupe, Geoffrey of Monmouth, and Cambridge's Arthurian Foundation Myth', *Medium Ævum* 72 (2003), pp. 63-81; on the Humber River in Arthurian story, see Cedric E. Pickford, 'The River Humber in French Arthurian Romances', *The Legend of Arthur in the Middle Ages*, eds. P.B. Grout *et al.* (D.S. Brewer, 1983), pp. 149-59.

CHAPTER 6

A good introduction to the Celtic Arthur is *The Arthur of the Welsh*, eds. Rachel Bromwich, A.O.H. Jarman, and Brynley F. Roberts (University of Wales, 1991). Most British Saints' *Vitae* (defined as saints of British or Cornish origin, or Irish saints whose cults were influential in Britain) can be found in S. Baring-Gould and John Fisher, *Lives of British Saints*, 4 volumes (Honourable Society of Cymmrodorion, 1907-13). Further information on the Celtic saints can be found in Elissa Henken, *Traditions of the Welsh Saints* (D.S. Brewer, 1987) and *The Welsh Saints: A Study in Patterned Lives* (D.S. Brewer, 1991), and on Cornish saints in particular see Catherine Rachel John, *The Saints of Cornwall: 1500 Years of Christian Landscape* (Tabb House, 2001). For more on Derfel and his parish, another good source is Tristan Gray Hulse, 'Three Saints, Two Wells and a Welsh Parish', in *The Holy Wells Journal* 6 (1998). On Cornwall's place in England, see Mark Stoyle, *West Britons: Cornish Identities and the Early Modern British State* (University of Exeter, 2002); Henry Jenner, *King Arthur and Cornwall* (Oakmagic, 1996) republishes two important articles on Arthurian place-names and on the history of Tintagel.

Index